Ordered this on Amazon

PRAISE FOR LEFT

"*LEFT* is a raw, well-written account of a heart-rending journey filled with gospel hope. Readers will find their own stories, in big or small ways, reflected in Jonathan's account of a young man seeking in everything what he could only find in Jesus."

- **J.D. GREEAR**, Lead Pastor, The Summit Church, and author of *Gaining by Losing, Jesus, Continued,* and *Gospel*

"The divorce epidemic has ripped through our culture, and even our churches. Those harmed the worst are the children of divorce. In this book, Jonathan Edwards speaks as one who experienced this hurt. He offers wise, gospel-focused counsel. If you've been through the pain of divorce, or if you know someone who has, this book is for you."

- **RUSSELL D. MOORE**, President, Ethics & Religious Liberty Commission, and author of *Onward*

"Powerful. Strong. Brutally honest. Heart wrenching. Healing. Hopeful. These are the words that come to my mind after reading *LEFT*. Married to a lovely lady whose story is similar in many ways to Jonathan's, I have seen both the pain a fallen world inflicts on so many when abandoned by a parent(s), and I have seen the healing that comes through Jesus and a relationship with a perfect Heavenly

Father. This is a book I could not put down. Neither will you."

> - **DANIEL L. AKIN**, President, Southeastern Baptist Theological Seminary, and author of *Engaging Exposition*

"*LEFT* is a raw and riveting series of reflections on life in the wake of parental abandonment. Those who have been through similar circumstances will find in Jonathan an articulate voice for this particular pain. Those who have not been through this experience will find a window into how best to minister and serve their friends from broken families. "

> - **TREVIN WAX**, Managing Editor of *The Gospel Project*, and author of *Gospel-Centered Teaching* and *Counterfeit Gospels*.

"A careful balancing act of narrative and memoire, staccato sentences ripe with good theology, Edwards leaves no pretty picture of life after divorce. Jonathan is real about the struggles. He confesses, he wrestles, he preaches, he stumbles. He is not the Puritan, but in *LEFT* we see that he does understand a little something about sinners in the hands of a faithful God."

> - **LORE FERGUSON WILBERT**, Writer at sayable.net and Director of Community & Formation at Park Church, Denver.

"When you open the pages of *LEFT*, you peer into the heart of anyone who has ever been abandoned by a parent. With raw emotion and haunting honesty, Jonathan Edwards poignantly pens of the lingering longing and gnawing ache that occurs when a parent leaves, and leads the reader to a place of healing and hope. If you have been left by a parent, you will see yourself in Jonathan's words and know that you are not alone. If you have a loved-one that is struggling with being left as a child, you will have a better understanding of the heart wounded by parental abandonment."

> - **SHARON JAYNES**, Best-selling author of *The Power of a Woman's Words* and *Your Scars are Beautiful to God*

"Some call this generation "the fatherless generation." And rightly so. If not orphaned, countless children are functionally fatherless. Abuse, abandonment, and neglect are all too familiar experiences for today's youth. These experiences are devastating. But there's hope. Jonathan points us to the fountain of hope and love in *LEFT*. By taking truth to struggle, Jonathan shows us that Jesus's grace sufficiently strengthens, sustains, and satisfies the believer in the midst of his or her grief and hardship."

> - **TONY MERIDA**, Lead Pastor, Imago Dei Church, and author of *Ordinary, Faithful Preaching,* and *Proclaiming Jesus*

"Concussed by his dad's leaving, Edwards narrates the particular, detailed miseries that he experienced as a boy, a teen, and an adult. But there is a turning, and his mother's love points him to the One who can heal, forgive and fill. To read *LEFT* is to grieve, but also to marvel anew at the Redeemer."

> - **GLENN LUCKE**, President, Docent Research Group

"In *LEFT* my friend Jonathan Edwards provides a biblically-informed, heartfelt, and pastoral book about the existential realities of divorce. This is a moving and helpful book. Highly recommended."

> - **BRUCE ASHFORD**, Provost, Southeastern Baptist Theological Seminary, and author of *One Nation Under God* and *Every Square Inch*

"From the very first page I was struck by the importance of *LEFT*. How many millions of kids have tried to make sense of their feelings of abandonment? Edwards takes the reader through the raw agony of rejection, the searing pain of loss and the brokenhearted emotions of a boy deprived of a father. Yet he has made a startling and redemptive move in writing this book. Rather than wallow around assigning blame, Jonathan works through the tragedy until he finds the peace of Jesus Christ. Forgiveness and healing find their way into his story and at the end he offers hope and a future to all those who still fight to keep their heads above water, never quite able to let go of their hurt or be rid of the nagging question, "What if?" Everyone knows someone who needs to read this."

- **DAVID HORNER**, Senior Pastor, Providence Baptist Church, and author of *When Missions Shapes the Mission*

"If a father could read this, he would nail his shoes to the floor. *LEFT* puts words to the experience and feelings of everyone who has lost a parent. Simply put, what Edwards says is so raw and so real, you will wonder how God could ever, ever heal a father-shaped hole in anyone's heart. But He can and He does. If losing a parent is part of your story, you will be so grateful for this book."

- **PAULA RINEHART**, Marriage and Family Counselor, and author of *Strong Women, Soft Hearts* and *Sex and the Soul of a Woman*

"Some stories inform. Others transform. Jonathan Edwards weaves a story that opens eyes to the dark world of kids left behind by abandoning parents. The winsome, well-written story telling in *LEFT* is much needed in the Christian community; for while Edwards exposes the seeming hopelessness of some divorces, he does not leave the reader in that state of hopelessness. Instead, he offers a way out, a way up. He offers the same hope to his readers that he has found himself in Jesus. He is empathetic. As the husband of a wonderful woman who was left by her own father, I have lived his story by proxy. As a Christian theologian I am hopeful that Jonathan's message will be heard in homes, coffee shops, and churches where hurting is real."

- **STEVE MCKINION**, Professor of Theology and Patristics, Southeastern Baptist Theological Seminary, and editor of *Life and Practice in the Early Church*

"*LEFT* is a journey in both the agony of abandonment and the joy of finding true healing in the saving work of Jesus Christ. Jonathan Edwards writes with a compelling and fresh style that draws the reader into the rawness of emotions and the intricacies of the movements of the heart through one of the most painful trials a person can experience—being left by a parent. This book will be a profound help to all who read it—both those who need the same kind of healing that God has worked in Jonathan's heart, and those who yearn to show compassion to others in that same situation."

> - **ANDREW DAVIS**, Senior Pastor, First Baptist Durham, and author of *An Infinite Journey*

"In *LEFT*, Jonathan Edwards does something that is hard to do; take us through the storm of divorce and abandonment, show us the ugly aftermath, and carry us into the hope of a bright tomorrow that only Christ can bring. To get there, Jonathan must tear into some old wounds for our benefit and for the benefit for those yet to travel this lonely, often puzzling journey. Out of the stark reality of brokenness comes hope and out of the despair of a difficult past comes a future of promise. If you have been on this road or know someone currently walking it, *LEFT* is both a reminder of the destruction we can bring to each other and the promise that those scars can become markers toward a joyful next step.

> - **STEVE TURNER**, Director of Campus Mobilization, North American Mission Board

"Jonathan writes with an honesty that will resonate deeply in the hearts of all who know what it's like to be disappointed, disillusioned and discouraged. In this candid, soul-searching memoir, Edwards exposes his struggles to make sense of the pain and loss he experienced in his father's abandonment. Ultimately, *LEFT* points to the hope found in God, our heavenly Father, who will never leave or abandon His children."

> - **GWEN SMITH**, Speaker, Songwriter, and author of *Broken into Beautiful* and co-author of *Knowing God by Name* and *Trusting God*

FROM THOSE WHO WERE LEFT...

LEFT echoes what I've often felt, thought, and wondered about my own broken background, but have never really had the courage to say, the humility to admit or the words to express. Like other broken homes the book describes, the home I grew up in was wrought with financial instability, emotional instability, and an overall atmosphere which bred an insecurity about who I was. Interestingly and perhaps unexpectedly, this stemmed from the parent that chose to raise us, but was never really there for us. My dad, after having been physically, mentally, and emotionally abused by my mother, was kicked out of his own house when I was a toddler. For me I don't know what it's like to grow up with a mom that's supportive and encouraging of everything you achieve or want to accomplish. Any memories of what little love and support she showed to me are drowned out by years of unbridled anger and criticism. Fortunately, my dad worked around my mom to be more loving, supportive, encouraging, and gentle well beyond what my mom could muster. My personal path of healing and recovery is still ongoing, but after reading *LEFT* I'm encouraged and reminded of the fact that the only way one can fully recover spiritually, mentally, and emotionally from the effects of a broken background is found in the saving and restorative work of a loving, sovereign God and His Son, Jesus Christ.

- NATHAN, 26

LEFT carries a huge burden, not just for the author, but for many of those who will read it. Jonathan does a great job breaking down the impact of what happens spiritually to a fatherless son while at the same time displaying God's love as the only foundation that will hold that child up. This book relates to those who have had a parent walk out on them and as a result, been left on their own to fight the daily spiritual battle against the memories of a past they wish to recreate. At the same time, this book gives those same children hope and comfort in our heavenly Father who will always be the sleeping bag that provides them safety no matter how bad the storm was or will ever be. My father left when I was eight due to an alcohol addiction. In the wake of all of it, God used my grandmother to fill in. No young boy should have to learn how to be a man from a 68-year old woman. However, I am thankful and blessed God used her and even more thankful and blessed that I found the heavenly Father through it all. If you grew up in a fatherless home, this book will point you to the Ultimate Father.

- BRYAN, 38

I am grateful for this book. My hope is that it will be widely read by the lonely and desperate hearts that feel like no one understands their abandonment. Jonathan is a wise, empathetic voice that points us to another who walked the lonely road of rejection: Jesus. As a woman with a father that rejected me and an alcoholic mother, I believed I must be unlovable. It wasn't until my 30s that I allowed God, through my own broken marriage, to mend my heart and free me from bondage. In *LEFT,* Jonathan's story gives this same hope, that though abandonment scars, Jesus heals.

- WHITNEY, 35

LEFT is a beautiful example of God's strength, sovereignty, and redemptive power in the midst of human weakness and pain. It's an honest and deeply personal reflection of hurt and confusion that finds its ultimate healing in the finished work of Christ. Jonathan's story will resonate with anyone who has experienced the pain of broken family relationships, and it points us back to the only Father who can redeem and restore. For me personally, this book was a powerful reminder that my joy and my identity are not dependent on my family's circumstances, but rooted in Christ, who is the ultimate demonstration of God's unconditional love for me. Our families may fail us (and we may fail our families), but God is faithful to His Word and relentless in His loving pursuit of us. He meets us in the middle of the mess, in the midst of the grief and pain, and gives us hope. For those who are trying to make sense of a loss, this book is where the hard and painful realities of life meet the love and grace of a Savior who one day will wipe every tear from our eyes.

- **KATY, 25**

Growing up as a kid in a single-parent home looks a million different ways, each one with their own story of heartache and longing. The emotions one experiences are varied, complex, and deep. In *LEFT* Jonathan explores the buried, even extremely painful and resonating fallout of how this has influenced his understanding of self as well as his relationship with God. These pages are filled with a raw and introspective look at the far-reaching effects of fatherlessness. Yet the ultimate response to this book is neither despair nor pity. On the contrary these personal experiences leave you pondering what it means to find joy, forgiveness, and even hope in a perfect heavenly Father. I'm grateful for Jonathan conveying this story not only to remind himself of the comfort he's found in Christ but also to remind us, regardless of our upbringing, that we all have access through Jesus to an ever-present, endless, and overwhelming source of peace and love through Jesus.

- **ETHAN, 36**

The raw and real emotion of *LEFT* brought back memories from my childhood that I haven't visited in a long time. The words in this book were, just as it describes, shovels that uncovered the messiness from my childhood that was lived in the aftermath of my parents' divorce. I am thankful for the way Jonathan points and pushes the reader to the cross, but especially those readers who come from the broken-home background he describes. I am thankful how he encourages us to not shy away from the mess but rather to come to the foot of the cross knowing that we are washed clean. This book is much needed in the culture today where broken families and single-parent homes are an epidemic that leave children in the wake of their family's destruction. Thankfully in *LEFT*, that destruction of growing up in a broken family is filtered through the lens of truth that restoration is coming and causes us to look to our faithful Provider when our families fail to provide what we need.

- **MICHELLE, 24**

I honestly started reading *LEFT* and could not put it down. Over the years I've often wondered if people struggled with divorce the way I have, and if being in a fatherless home raised the same emotions and struggles that I seemed to deal with constantly. So often over the years I have found myself reminiscing on thoughts and memories of my dad. I've wondered what it would have been like to have had him in the house with my mom, and what if I had gone through life without the pain and suffering of being in a broken home. Like Jonathan's story, I have constantly sought after my dad's satisfaction and love and have constantly been disappointed. I have been hurt, and I have hit my low point several times, but this book has brought me some perspective and realization.

I've come to realize that I have learned more about myself and my relationship with Christ when I was at my lowest points in life. I believe God used my parents' divorce to show me his unconditional love and glory. He has put certain people in my life to show me what it means to be a godly man and a loving father because I was never given that in my own home. This just goes to show you how God hears us and how he provides. It's only through Jesus and my eternal Father that I will truly find and experience true satisfaction, and my earthly father will never come close to loving me the way my savior does. I haven't talked to my dad for some time now, and after reading this book and meditating in prayer, I've decided to contact him and forgive him.

- HOLT, 21

As a father myself, struggling to deal with the emotional wreckage left in the wake of my own father who didn't seem to care, *LEFT* was just what I needed. Jonathan, through the telling of his own childhood stories, showed me that the pain I felt many years ago doesn't disappear overnight or even over time if left unresolved. Jonathan's story placed me in a position to confront the pain in my heart and taught me much about the relationship between my present struggles and the scars of my past. Dealing with those scars as I read this book left me with a greater appreciation of some foundational truths in my life. Through all of the pain, there is hope. Through all of the loneliness, there is love. Jesus loves me in the way I always hoped my father would. I am enough for him, and that is enough for me.

- JOHNSON, 33

Unfortunately, the words that Jonathan has written are shared with many men of this generation, the generation before, and regrettably the next generation. Jonathan's story is my story. Though my father was physically present, he still was absent in almost every other way. What Jonathan has done is capture what life is like when a father walks out. What he leaves behind. What my father left behind was a marriage, spouse, daughter, son, a family. And that is something as a man that affected me, that makes me question what life could, should have looked like.

That's why reading *LEFT* was difficult, because it brought up so many feelings, emotions, and memories. Memories that I never knew existed, or ones that I had tried to forget. But Jonathan didn't end with hopelessness and living as a victim of his circumstance. He tells a story of a father who truly loves, never walks out, and who is always present. God in His great mercy carried Jonathan, showed him what real love of a father looks like. That's where *LEFT* differs from other stories. This book points to Christ—to hope. Because those memories of my father leaving, walking out are difficult, but reading Jonathan's words tell me I am not alone. There are others like me. There is a Father who loves me and allows me to love my family, my future kids, my future wife, and my father.

- CHASE, 28

For anyone affected by the brokenness of divorce and family dysfunction, *LEFT* offers more than just words; it offers the experience of being completely heard and understood. As you read, you'll find these pages tell your story, and so many stories of kids all across our country. America has become a culture where self-satisfaction is more important than keeping your word and raising a child you brought into this world. This book gives an entire generation of children "left on the front porch" a loud, clear, and necessary voice that deserves to be heard. Jonathan leads readers back to the dark places in their past and helps them come head to head with the pain, but doesn't leave them there. More than just feeling understood, readers will feel empowered by the gospel to move out of despair, anger, and resentment. *LEFT* offers us the message we need to set us free from the marring of being abandoned: the story of God who went through abandonment for us and offers us the ability to forgive. If you want to feel heard, understood, and more importantly set free from the wounds of divorce, you'll find your story intersecting with God's in the pages of *LEFT*.

- ASHLEY, 28

LEFT takes a deep look into the messiness that results from a broken home and the stages of emotion that follow, yet also tells a story of hope in that while we may be left, we are not alone. I related with many aspects of this book. There were many times I felt transported back to my childhood and could feel many of the emotions, like the shameful lunches, and the fear of my dad, and the weirdness of two Christmases and the never being "good enough."

Yet all broken homes are different, and while my experience was very different than Jonathan's, it was comforting to read and understand that like us, there are many others who experience hurt, pain, and wounds that result from broken homes. But in the end, of course, it's always awesome to be reminded that Jesus is bigger than it all, and that He is ultimate hope and restoration.

- JENNA, 27

There's a malaise that has infected our culture for decades. Children, preteens, and teens growing up in families amputated through the abandonment of a parent or both. You can hear their muffled cries through a pillow as they try to sleep at night. You can see the devastation on their faces in blank stares in the classroom. You can sense a general feeling of being unwell from the young couple who has no idea how to be a husband or a wife. Forsaken boys and girls grow up confused as to who they are and what they're to do. Constantly searching for someone or something to take care of them. This was my story.

LEFT exposed the lingering atrophy that still exists in my own soul as I battle with the wounds caused by an absent parent. Each chapter took me further and further into the hurts of my past. There were many times I wanted to stop reading. Memories of pain and fear almost suffocated me. But in my anguish I found healing. That's how the gospel works though. Paradoxical. The way down is the way up.

Jonathan's rigorous honesty has opened the door for those afflicted by the pandemic of desertion to make sense of their stories and to piece together the wreckage of their past. To see the upheaval of their childhoods as a means to find perfect love and acceptance in Jesus- who went through hell so we wouldn't have to. I'm praying others will walk with Jonathan as they begin to tell their own stories. Because that's the only way those affected by the disorder of being left will begin to find healing.

- JUSTIN, 35

Left.

the struggle to make sense of life
when a parent leaves

JONATHAN C. EDWARDS

FOREWORD BY

TREVIN WAX

LEFT: The Struggle to Make Sense of Life When a Parent Leaves

Jonathan Edwards
www.NotThePuritan.com

Published by Rainer Publishing
www.RainerPublishing.com

ISBN 978-0692714225

Printed in the United States of America

To my mom, Pat Edmondson.

You are the most wonderful person I have ever known or will meet. Thank you for being such a godly mother. Thank you for showing me what it looks like to truly entrust yourself into the hands of our beloved Savior. You mean the world to me. I will never be able to repay you for all that you did and continue to do to love and care for us, your children. You made sure we knew that you loved us with every bone in your body. More importantly, you made sure we understood that, unlike our father and your former husband, Christ will never abandon us. Thank you for showing me that what Christ has done for us is such good and glad news.

CONTENTS

L|F

•••• •

FOREWORD
ABSENT

by Trevin Wax

Parents are important.

We know this. We recognize the need for a solid education, a stable home, and parents who are present and involved in the lives of their children.

But too often we think of parenting in generic terms, and thereby minimize the distinctive contribution of a father to a family.

How important is fatherhood?

Sometimes, you don't know how important something is until it's missing.

A few years ago, my wife and I were caught up in the popular television drama, *Lost*. The intriguing storyline and compelling characters had us coming back every week to see what would take place next.

Midway through the series, I was struck by how many of the main characters had "daddy issues." Much of the ongoing struggle and personal conflict was traced back to the characters' unresolved issues with their fathers—some who'd been present (and bad) and others who were absent.

Most disturbing was how, in some cases, the anger toward fathers led to patricide. *Lost* presented a frightening picture of what can take place when the biblical vision of fatherhood is missing. Suffering, anger, pain, and violence followed a father's abdication of responsibility.

Flash forward a few years, and I'm sitting in my living room with a group of college students. We're talking about the subject matter for a new book I am writing—a work of fiction that teaches theological truth in story form. As I talk with them about the main character, a young college student struggling with big questions about Christianity, they advise me:

There needs to be a dad problem.

I was puzzled. But they insisted.

If you want this book to resonate with lots of guys, the dad needs to be absent. College students will relate.

There needs to be a dad problem.

Those of us who seek to proclaim the gospel today cannot ignore the massive implications of a distorted vision of fatherhood—fathers who have failed or fathers who have left. Due to fickle fathers and distant dads, our culture's view of God has been massively affected by the failures of our fathers.

And yet, the gospel becomes all the sweeter when it gains a foothold in the heart of someone longing for a Father who never fails. A Father whose gracious love for His creation led Him to reveal Himself as our Creator and Redeemer. In the gospel, we encounter a Son who was abandoned that we might be accepted, cast out that we might be brought in, crucified that we might be raised.

Jonathan Edwards understands the pain of fatherlessness. He also understands the sweetness of the gospel. This book is a raw and riveting series of reflections on life in the wake of parental abandonment.

If you are fatherless, you'll resonate.

If you are like me and you've been blessed with an earthly father who faithfully models our heavenly Father, you will find this book to be a window into how best to minister and serve our friends from broken families.

Here is a book that gives us a taste of a particular kind of pain, a pain felt by those who are seeking to remember what's good and forget what's bad, cherish the true and discard the false, love and forgive . . . and hope again.

● ● ● ●　　●

INTRODUCTION
MESSY

Digging a hole is tough. It's a lot of work. And you certainly don't want to be doing it in your Sunday best.

Because digging a hole is messy.

Your hands get filthy with dirt and it gets under your fingernails and covers your clothes and gets on your face. Even if it's a small hole for a small plant in the flower bed right in front of your steps leading up to your front porch. You put your garden gloves on and maybe a little apron and get your tiny shovel and the small pad for your knees and you get to work.

And you get dirty.

Because digging a hole is messy. It's messy and it's interesting.

It's interesting because holes come in all different shapes and sizes. Some take enormous amounts of time to create and others not so much.

Some holes are created in an instant, and some take days, weeks, and months. Some small holes might not take as much time but they can be a lot more work just as well.

The time it takes is directly connected to what you're using to make your hole. You could be using a tiny garden shovel or a multi-ton excavator with a giant shovel arm extension. You could be using a shovel with a sharp point at the end, or one with a square head, perfect for shoveling snow.

Whatever the tool of choice, all of these were meant to do the same thing: make holes. And while that remains true, they weren't all meant for every kind of hole. You wouldn't break ground for the construction of a new building or collection of offices with a garden spade.

But yes, shovels are made to dig.

It just comes down to what kind of hole is being dug.

Have you ever realized how certain days on the calendar can be excellent shovels concerning our past?

Certain days throughout the year dig up all kinds of things: memories, feelings, emotions, laughter, depression, sadness, joy, and heartbreak. The thing is, different days are different kinds of shovels. One day in the summer could be a tiny little green garden shovel that reminds you of your first kiss that happened the year before.

Great memory.

One dug up by the numbers on your watch or computer or tablet letting you know what day it is.

Emotional.

Fun.

A small hole.

But other days are different. Other number combinations for different dates and times aren't your typical shovel from Lowe's or Home Depot. Other days are big, bright green John Deere diggers and dumpers.

Excavators.

These days go deep. They go big. They excavate. They break through layers of soil. They bring up memories and days and emotions that are deep beneath the surface of the soul. These days are beyond the visible smiles and laughter and glossed eyes. These days hurt. These days are complicated.

They dig up and take us back and make us remember.

Even when we don't want to.

Because digging a hole is messy.

It's messy when we look at the calendar and realize it's been 11 years since he called. It's been three years since she died. It's been five years since the accident, or since the diagnosis came in, or since they left, or since the operation. We look down and our hands are messy. Our shoes and pants and shirt are stained with the dirt from our past.

Because it's messy to relive and re-experience messiness.

We get dirty when our holes get re-dug.

For me, this is my dad's birthday. This day digs up all kinds of soil and plunges me right back into a huge pit. This day reminds me that he's not here. It reminds me that he left. It reminds me that I haven't spoken to him in 11 years. It makes me sad and it makes me ache. It makes me hate messiness. It makes me wish things were just normal and life was squeaky clean.

And just four days before this hole gets dug another one opens up and more dirt gets shoveled. Because that day reminds my wife that, for her too, it's been 11 years since she has spoken with her dad.

And that day is her John Deere.

But not because he left and he won't talk to her. But because 10 years ago on that day, her dad left this earth, losing his fight against leukemia.

And that's a big hole.

A deep hole.

A hole that we wish never had been dug.

But it's there. And some days are like that. Some days are the giant shovels that dig out the earth and the soil that started to fill holes and cover certain aspects of our messy past that we keep buried. And that's what happens on days like that. They all are processed differently and dealt with in different ways because we all look at our holes differently from different angles. Some jump in and others stand up top and look down. But the holes are there for all of us. And it's tough when you know those days are coming. You glance at the calendar from a week out, maybe two, and realize that you're going to have to face that Thursday.

You're going to have to deal with the dirt that gets unearthed.

You're going to have to get messy.

And what do we do on these days?

We get angry. We get sad. We get bitter. We cry. We yell. We yearn.

And we hurt.

Because life is messy and it's not always how we want it to be.

And we don't like messiness. We like to be clean and free from dirt and for everything to be where it should be and for nothing to go wrong. We want everything to be perfect, not messed up. We want to be smiling the whole time and to enjoy our experiences and to be happy. We want everything to be picture perfect—just like a wedding day.

Weddings are not considered messy days. They are clean, proper, fancy, perfect, well-dressed, and dolled up. Flowers are perfect. Cakes are perfect. Clothes are perfect. A wedding day is the one day in our lives where we all think that nothing should go wrong. It's that one special day. It shouldn't rain, and the food should be right, and the flowers should be placed perfectly, and all the pictures should be great, and no one should forget where to stand.

The perfect day.

No messiness.

But when we look at what marriage is, when we turn to the Scriptures, we understand that marriage is but a symbol of the ultimate relationship between God and us, His people, His bride. And in this marriage, we see that God Himself, the Creator of the flowers that overflow every room and chair and table at weddings, the cotton made to produce the dresses and the suits, the trees for the programs, the chemicals for the makeup, the very Creator who made all these, chose for the joining of Himself to His bride to be something not perfect, but messy.

In the very beginning, in the creation account in Genesis, after God made His glorious creation and after forming man and knowing it wasn't the best for Him to be alone, He did something. He formed from Adam's side a helper.[1]

Eve.

She was his mate and his companion. But after this, after their union, we don't know how long, but we know after their union they were deceived and they chose a life for themselves and chose their desires over their God.[2]

They chose selfishness.

They chose idolatry.

And here we see not only the first instance of sin, but also the very intricate nature of sin and its effects.

They hide.

They fear.

They blame.

They're ashamed.

But God comes.

He confronts.

He explains.

He renders the consequences for their actions. And the first step he takes is what? He clothes them. He covers their shame. And this isn't some fine, Vera Wang gown, this is fig leaves.

Attractive? No.

Messy? Yes.

You see, this clothing that He gave them was a mere temporary fix. We know this because in chapter 3, before dishing out punishments, He dishes out promise. In Genesis 3:15 we see the promise to one day destroy evil.3 And guess what? He is going to do this by getting messy and getting his hands dirty.

Centuries later, a baby will be born and God Himself will throw Himself into the mess, putting on what? Human skin. Human clothes. Marred clothes. Messy clothes.

And so to provide what is needed for the ultimate marriage of God and His bride, His people, He had to get messy. To provide what was needed for restoration and renewal; for recreation and the defeat of death; for triumph over brokenness and hurt and sin and messiness, God plunged into messiness. Without the messiness, there's no restoration and there's no wedding when Christ returns and all things are made new.

Without the messiness of Jesus, we're still wearing our fig leaves. We're still messy with no promise or hope of being made clean and having our holes filled. While our lives are messy and circumstances and situations on this broken earth hurt and poke and make us uncomfortable and make us resent messiness, we need to find joy in it, knowing that it is through messiness that our hope of God putting all things back together will come to pass.

So let us be joyful. Let us be grateful in the midst of our mess that because God Himself came down and entered into our mess, and our sin, and our shame, we now have the joy and the gracious opportunity to be restored and to be renewed and made clean. Because that's what we need. That's great news amidst our brokenness, our imperfections, and our flaws.

Let us rejoice that the most important wedding of all time will be the most wondrous and the most regal. And it will all be about the Groom.

And let us keep in mind that it is possible only because the Groom Himself became messy.

And that is good news for messy people.

That's what we wait for. We long, and we ache to be made new and for all creation to be restored when Jesus comes again. He will wipe away tears and heartbreak and loneliness and join together his family.

So just as we wait for that Day,4 and just as we continue to live in the brokenness of creation, I urge you to do that with this book. Persevere. Press on.

Make it to the end.

Don't let the messiness and all the dirty laundry sideline you and keep you from moving on. I know it's messy and dirty, and I know that this mess will unearth many things for many hurting people. But don't leave. There's great joy in the end, just as there will be for us who believe that Jesus is who he says he is and that he did come to do what he promised he would do.

Only He promises new life and hope and joy and peace among life's greatest of voids.

All because he took on himself the death and decay that began in the garden, swallowing up the emptiness from our sin and shame and pain when he hung on the cross. All because he became messy to clean up messiness for good.

And only Jesus can do this.

Only he can fill our holes.

But not with just dirt.

Life.

L|1

●●●● ●

CHAPTER ONE
EMPTY

In my brother's house there's a bookshelf. It's nothing fancy. It's just a dark-brown, tall, wooden piece of furniture. It's plain. It's simple.

It's a bookshelf.

This bookshelf is older than I am. It has survived every house and every move and every apartment that my family has occupied since the early 1980s. It has some miles on it. It has done some traveling. It has history. It has stories. The thing it doesn't have is books.

And it's a bookshelf.

With all these things, the element that rises above every description and characteristic of this big brown rectangular box is its memories. This bookshelf has memories. Lining every one of the five wooden planks that make up its shelves is memory after memory after memory.

Memories from a time long ago.

Memories from an inescapable past.

This bookshelf, with all its contents, is worth a good bit of money. On every shelf is collector memorabilia. From Bo Jackson and Deion Sanders figurines to encased boxes of the '92 and '96 Dream Teams. The bottom few shelves are lined with album after album after album after album of collectors' cards. And this bookshelf hasn't changed. Nothing on the shelves has ever moved the slightest centimeter from its original spot.

Never dusted.

Never cleaned.

Always the same.

And on the very top shelf is a box of Wheaties.

This box of Wheaties was purchased some time during 1990. How do I know? On the front of the box is a picture of the Air Man himself, Michael Jordan. Jordan, during his playing years, was featured on the front of General Mills' Breakfast of Champions on several occasions, each having its own year. But this one, the one on my brother's bookshelf, is from 1990.

And it is unopened.

That's right.

On the top of my brother's bookshelf is a 25 year-old unopened box of Wheaties. I can't imagine how gross a bowl of that cereal would be.

The thing is, all these items on this bookshelf are very different. Cards. Figurines. Trophies. Placards. Displays. Cereal. Yet, while they are all very different in form, they all contain the very same intangible quality. The items on these shelves all have one characteristic that binds them together, that joins every single one of them, making them all of the same value to my big brother.

All these things connect back to our dad.

Throughout our childhood, card collecting was the thing my dad and brother did together. They'd spend weekends at card shows, hunting for something worthwhile. Maybe a limited edition Penny Hardaway card or a rare Starting Lineup figure. All these things on his shelf point back to all those times. They aren't collectors' items to him.

They're memories.

And sure, an unopened box of Wheaties is worth more than an opened one. I get that. But that Wheaties box is doing more than just sitting there for my big brother. That Wheaties box is preserving memories and stories with my dad far better than it is keeping those crunchy, brown flakes fresh.

And it is.

It does.

It's not about Wheaties. It's not about Bo Jackson or Deion Sanders or the Dream Team or L'il Penny. It's about a time that is gone.

A time that doesn't exist anymore.

A time that gets a little bit further back in history with every day that passes.

Every time my brother passes this bookshelf, it rewinds his life. It takes him away from the present and into the past. It shows him, that no matter what is going on that day, no matter what circumstances say, no matter how long it's been, no matter how or what or when or where, this bookshelf screams to him that his dad isn't a myth.

He exists.

He was around.

He is real.

He is a person.

And that's what this bookshelf is. It's a daily, tangible sign that our family wasn't always this way. It shows him that our dad wasn't always this far away. It shows him that he was near.

He was close.

He was here.

Each of us has our own signs that he was around. In my living room, there's a book signed by my dad, keeping safe a note that he wrote to me in March of 2004. The book is a modern history of Saturday Night Live. The night he penned his note I had the opening of a play that was basically an episode of Saturday Night Live for my high school. My dad couldn't make the official curtain drop but showed up at the rehearsal and gave me the book with the note.

When I was in high school, being on Saturday Night Live was my dream. But I don't keep this book for that. It's not about Will Ferrell or Jimmy Fallon. It's about my dad. It's more than just a book.

It's a reminder.

My sister has a closet full of polar bear stuffed animals, all in black trash bags, stored at my mom's house.

Stored.

Not displayed.

Not sold.

Each of these bears, just like a bookshelf full of collectors' items or just one single book with a short note, represents for her a time.

A season.

A year.

A gift.

A person.

My dad gave her every single one. And they don't represent childhood.

They represent him.

SIGNATURES

There's this picture in my office.

Much like my brother's bookshelf, it's nothing to talk extensively about. It's definitely nothing that Thomas Kinkade spent his time on and it's nothing close to Rob Bell's *Velvet Elvis* that was in his basement back in 2005. It's just a photograph. It's probably a picture similar to ones many people have in their house or somewhere in their attic or workspace. It's simply a small, framed picture of my wife and me on our wedding day surrounded by signatures on a white matte background. Some big. Some small. Some from people I know and some from people I don't. Whenever I find myself looking at all of the handwriting and all the names, my mind floods with memories, making endless connections to so many different people and so many different seasons of life. I am reminded of stories and inside jokes. I remember specific conversations, being drawn into past and present relationships and highs and lows and faces and places and all sorts of emotions.

All of this from signatures.

Tiny names on a white matte that frames a picture of my wife and me.

When I look at this frame and all the signatures surrounding the small, 5"x7" picture, it seems so cluttered. It seems so messy and so jumbled. Hundreds of little signatures crowding this small picture. There are names everywhere and in all different sizes and shapes.

And although this white matte is filled to its borders in black ink, it's empty.

Amidst the clutter and claustrophobia, there's so much room. There's so much missing from the little space among all these signatures.

Signatures from friends.

Signatures from aunts.

Signatures from uncles.

Signatures from mentors.

Signatures from grandparents.

Signatures from brothers.

Signatures from sisters.

Signatures from mothers.

All but one.

Even though I know it's not there, I always stop and look for my dad's name. But I don't find it. No matter how long I look, no matter how many times I look, and no matter how much I want it to be there, it doesn't show up. I can't find his name. And no matter how many signatures crowd together, it will always be missing one. It will always have a hole. It will always have room for one more. It will always have an empty space that wasn't filled with a name.

His.

It seems that staring at this picture jolts me out of the present moment and into another one just like my brother's bookshelf does for him. Looking at this picture and these names, desperately searching for "Love, Dad", takes me back to my wedding day. I think about the suits and the food and the pictures and the flowers and the cake and the numbers and all the different details. I think about how there were too many people in our wedding party. I think about how there were too many people at the rehearsal dinner. I think about how there wasn't enough food. I think about how there were too many drawn out monologues with the microphone and how the stories lasted too long and how people were ready to leave. I think about how there were too many pictures and too many poses.

But then I think about how I was one groomsman short.

I think about how there was time for one more toast.

I think about how I wanted one more picture.

I think about how there was room for one more at our table.

I think about how there was one person who didn't get to taste the fried chicken.

Right in the middle of the weekend's excess and abundance, there was shortage. Right in the midst of the fullness of the day's schedule, there was all the time in the world. Right when we thought there was too much, there wasn't enough.

And right next to joy and celebration was deep sadness and heartache.

It's because your dad is supposed to be at your wedding. He's supposed to be your best man. He's supposed to give a toast and say how proud he is of you. He's supposed to say how excited he is to be getting a new member of the family. He's supposed to make people laugh. He's supposed to be there to give you advice and calm your nerves. He's supposed to be there to hug you. He's supposed to be there to take pictures with you.

He is supposed to be there.

And when he's not, it hurts. Knowing he's not there cripples you. It makes you sick to your stomach. Knowing he's not there to hug you and stand beside you makes you want a hug from him even more. It makes looking back on your wedding day something difficult to do rather than a delight. It makes you wonder if he wanted to be there as much as you wanted him to be. It makes you think about where he is and what he's doing. And in the end, it reminds you of how much you miss him.

It makes a day full of so many things at the same time feel so very empty. And my wedding day wasn't the first time this emptiness showed up.

WHAT NOW

It was July of 1993.

I was 7.

I remember sitting in the living room with my brother and sister on our rust-colored floral couch. My mom and dad just told us they were splitting up, and I remember them saying this wasn't necessarily for good, but it was for our good and for our well-being. They said this was for the good of the family. They said it was best this way. They said they were not getting a divorce, but that they were separating for just a season.

For our benefit?

For *just* a season?

I remember being unable to comprehend why that clarification mattered. I'm seven years-old, my dad just told me he's moving out of the house and the rest of the family is moving into an apartment where he won't be living and won't be coming over to visit. A seven year-old can't see the difference in that because to a seven year-old, there is no difference. All I knew was that he was leaving and I wasn't going with him. I was the youngest of three. I was the baby, and all I wanted to know was where my daddy was going and when was he coming home. What was so important that he had to leave?

I felt like my heart was split in two and one half had been taken from me. I wanted to be a family again.

I wanted to *have* a family again.

I knew after this there was no more cutting the grass together.

There was no more crawling up in bed with him to read the morning paper and watch cartoons.

There were no more crosswords on Sunday mornings.

There was no more watching him shave.

There was no more him.

How was this for my good? How was his absence from my life a benefit to me? How was his not tucking me in at night and not driving me to my baseball games for the better? How was being picked up every now and then and driven to a hotel room to stay with him for one night the best option? I didn't want to do my homework in a hotel room with him. I wanted to eat dinner and do my homework with him at home, as a family, like a normal kid. Did they want me to believe that his decision to leave was for my good to cover up that it was actually for his good and his good alone? Telling me it was in my best interest seemed to hide what was really happening; he wanted out, he was done, and he was calling it off.

But how can you call off your family? By telling me he was making the decision while thinking of me he disguised the real reason he was leaving - the reality that the decision was made for his own interests and gains. That is how I felt. From where I was standing on the porch while watching him pack up his car and pull out of the driveway, it seemed this decision was serving him a lot better than it was serving the rest of my family. Nothing seemed good on that front porch. I wasn't happy. I wasn't whole. I was standing there, immovable and unable to utter any sound. It wasn't long before he had a new job, a new girlfriend, a new hair color, new clothes, and new hobbies. But here we were, still the very same. Here I was, still hurting and still fatherless.

He just . . . moved on.

Sitting on the couch listening to his monologue all my mind could translate was

I'm sorry. It's just a lot better for me if I leave. It will be better because then I can quit pretending I want to be here. I've been a father for 13 years and a husband for 19. I've lost interest. I'm bored. I want to try new things. I want to have new experiences. Trust me, you will be fine. Let's shake hands and go our separate ways. I'll send a postcard.

What happened to family dinners and Friday movie nights with pizza? Didn't that mean anything to him? Was he not going to miss any of that? Was he not going to miss us? I couldn't bring myself to believe what happened. I couldn't bring myself to trust it.

Distrust rooted itself deep in my heart. I questioned whether or not my dad knew exactly what was happening to me. I doubted that he knew what my world looked like now and the intricate ways my heart was breaking. Life had taken such sudden, sharp, unexpected, and unpleasant turns. And when that happened, I found myself relegated to living in the fog of doubt and uncertainty. I felt so broken and so negatively affected by the decision made to split my family in two.

For children of divorce, this is tough to process because it does not make sense to us. We don't see this as logical. We *can't* see this as logical. We struggle to understand the reasoning that made divorce seem necessary. If a decision of such magnitude was made, leaving us terribly wrecked on the inside, it's hard to recover our trust. It's hard for us to believe in our family again. It's hard to believe in

a point,

a purpose,

a parent.

Because if we really were understood, if our needs were really important, we would still be a whole family. We wouldn't be with dad for Thanksgiving and with mom for Christmas. We wouldn't be without a concrete definition for what a family is, for what our family is. Our family would be easy to understand and easy to explain.

Our family would make sense to a child.

It would make sense to a 15 year-old.

It would make sense to a six year-old.

It would make sense to 24 year-old.

It would make sense to us.

And what makes sense is that mommy and daddy stay together, because we're a family and to us that is what families do. We believe they stay together. We believe they help us rather than hurt us. We believe families should make us feel better, not worse. But the truth of our stories is that this isn't the case. Our families don't make sense to us. Our families make us confused. They make us unsure. They make us doubt. They make us lose trust.

Because my father left my family.

And I will never forget it. I kept asking my mom where he was and why he wasn't home. I wanted to know why he wasn't eating dinner with us, and why his car wasn't in the driveway. It bothered me. It kept me up at night. I didn't know how to process being home and living life without him there. I remember feeling so vulnerable and exposed. I remember being so uncomfortable. I had so many questions and so many concerns. It was here that I was reluctantly introduced to the empty space that would begin making its way through every aspect of my life. This vacancy, this void, was everywhere.

As I began re-imagining life and attempting to re-learn what my days, nights, holidays, meals, tee-ball games, Saturday afternoons, bed times, and home was going to look like, there was so much of this empty space. It was taking over. There was space in the living room where his big, blue leather chair used to be. There was a space at the end of the table where he used to sit and tell us jokes and talk about his day and tell me to always eat over my plate. There was a space in the driveway next to mom's van where his light blue Honda Civic used to be parked. There was a space in his bathroom at his sink where his toothbrush and toothpaste and deodorant used to be. There was space next to mom in their bed where he used to sleep. There was space in new pictures and on the mantle at Christmas where his stocking used to hang and in the laundry basket where his dirty clothes used to be.

But his clothes weren't there. Our laundry basket didn't have any of his t-shirts or pants or socks. All the clothes in the basket were too small for him. We didn't have any daddy clothes to wash.

The days and months unfolded with this ever-present, physical emptiness forced to be tolerated by a mind too young to comprehend anything inside this new way of life. I didn't know what to say or how to act.

I just . . . existed.

It was a whole new world to me and this new world I was in was much different from the one Aladdin and Jasmine sang about. Normal became foreign. Everything was strange. Every day I woke up hoping it was all a dream, hoping that I'd run downstairs and there he'd be in his blue and white bathrobe with his brown leather slippers, drinking coffee and having breakfast doing his crossword. But once I woke up he was nowhere to be found and he left me nothing to help navigate and comprehend the hell I was in. He didn't leave me any instructions or guide to help me weather this monster of a storm that he created. I felt broken. I felt lost. I felt abandoned. There was no warning, nothing on the news to tell me where to go, or how to hide, or how to stay safe.

There was nothing to warn me that everything I knew, everything I called home and everything I called family, was going to shatter. And in the aftermath, there wasn't a class to take. There wasn't an instructional video to watch. It all just switched. One day he was there.

The next day he wasn't.

Just like that he was gone.

And just like that there I was.

Left.

I hurt for answers, clinching my fist while screaming into my pillow. I cried for them. I'd lie in my bunk bed, my mind racing, aching to know what happened. It was a mystery. A giant riddle. No matter how hard I tried, nothing helped. I found myself on my knees begging for some kind of deliverance. I just wanted to understand. I wanted to understand something that I don't think will ever make sense. I wanted to understand why families break and why parents leave. I wanted to understand why my family broke and why someone hadn't come to fix it.

I wanted to understand why I was not good enough.

Why was there this big empty space always lurking in our house?

What was I going to do with this big hole in my heart?

I stared at pictures of him. Stared at the way he was hugging me. Stared at the way he was smiling. Stared at his arm hair. His glasses. I wanted a hug. I wanted him to tickle me. I wanted to smell his cologne. I stared at him while my eyes leaked and my nose ran and my heart broke and I'd whisper to the picture

Where'd you go?

Was it my fault?

Did I do something wrong?

If I say I am sorry will you come back?

Are we going to see each other again?

Are you angry?

Is this a dream?

When are you coming home?

Why me?

I wanted to collapse. I wanted to disappear. If I yelled louder and cried harder would he come back? Would he hear me? If he could just hear me and see the pain and the agony my little heart was in he would come back. He would have to. Surely seeing his son in pain would make him not want to give up and would make him want to keep going and fight through whatever was going on. If only he could see. If only he knew.

He would fight for me, right?

He would fight for our family, wouldn't he?

I wanted my dad to suit up, put his armor on, and go to battle for us, his sons, his daughter, and his wife. I longed for him to go to war for the unity of our family. I wanted to be worth something to him. I wanted him to care, and I wanted everything to just go back to normal. The way that it used to be. I wanted . . .

A different life.

A different scenario.

No abandonment.

No yelling.

No lying.

No discouragement.

No affairs.

No illusions.

More love.

More quality time.

More hugs.

More goodnight kisses.

More affirmation.

More honesty.

More fun.

More reassurance.

More dedication.

More permanence.

CHRISTMAS PRESENCE

There was Buzz Lightyear sitting on the couch.

And so were Woody, Rex, Ham, and Slink.

It's because Pixar released *Toy Story* in November of 1995 and *Toy Story* action figures were the hot Christmas items. Woody and Buzz were at the top of my list. In the back of my mind, even as a 10 year-old, I thought maybe they would come to life like in the movie.

And there they sat on the couch in the living room of my grandma's house. Staring back at me from their plastic packaging. I tore open their boxes, while my brother and sister tended to their respective pieces of furniture containing their wish lists come true.

It was Christmas.

And we were together.

We were together because after dad left that first time in 1993, he came back to us several months later. He apologized. He wanted to be with us again. He wanted to be our dad again. He wanted our family to be what it was.

What we wanted it to be.

What we hoped it would be.

And so there we were. Together again. For Christmas.

Mom helped Grace Anne with her presents while dad helped us with ours. He'd take pictures of us ripping the wrapping off and screaming once we could see a tiny corner of the box letting us know that yes, we did get some new PJs. If anything amidst the holiday loot was packaged in that plastic that no human hand has ever been able to dismantle, dad would bring the scissors in and break through to the toy that I thought I would never get to touch.

He was good like that.

He always helped us.

Next to Woody and the *Toy Story* crew was a big box of LEGOS.

He and I spent the whole day side-by-side putting together an underwater city. The complexity and the detail were clearly beyond my age range, but I loved it. I loved that it was too hard for me to do on my own. I loved that he sat with me and helped me. It was the best, being with him that Christmas day in Grandmommy's living room. We assembled and fortified the underworld palace. His work clothes were his blue and white bathrobe classically coupled with his brown leather slippers and, without fail, his coffee by his side.

We prepped all the men for their underwater life. Gave them all their helmets and oxygen tanks and made sure they were ready to go.

They were all smiling.

It's the most remarkable thing about life in LEGO land, isn't it? It doesn't matter what was going on or what your job is or how much bumpy grass you have. It doesn't matter if you have brown hair, no hair, beard, or no beard. It doesn't matter if you're an astronaut or a policeman or a pirate or a prisoner or a deep-sea diver or Batman.

It doesn't matter.

You're yellow.

And you're smiling.

I felt like a giant LEGO man that Christmas, smiling the whole time. I was smiling when I went to sleep by the fire and when he tucked me in on Christmas Eve. I was smiling when we poured the milk and made the cookies and set them above the fireplace. I was smiling when I woke up the next morning and smiled the entire day.

And it wasn't because of his presents.

It was because of his presence.

But that Christmas shared with Woody and Buzz and a select few from the X-Men squad was the last Christmas five stockings would hang from the mantle.

From then, on there would always be room for one more stocking.

His long, slender red and white striped stocking never got put up again above that fireplace. If I had known that in the midst of those 1995 Christmas festivities, I would have done things differently. I would have forgotten about the LEGO city and the toys and the candy and the pajamas, and I would have simply snuggled with him. We could have sat by the fire and not said a word. Just us two.

Father.

And son.

After that you don't think much about Santa or toys. Your Christmas wish isn't for Santa to come down your chimney, it's for your dad to walk through the front door. You don't care what kind of shoes or skateboards or computers are in the living room waiting for you on the couch. None of it matters because you know the one thing on the top of your list, the one thing above all the toys and the games, is to have your family together again at Christmas. But deep down you know that it just won't happen. You know that Santa can't do that. He can't go down to his workshop and tell the elves to round up your dad.

It's because at Christmas, Santa is more of a reality to you than your dad is. The myth of Santa never goes away. It doesn't leave. It stays. It's always, without fail, intangibly, but tangibly, there.

A few years ago I met with a freshman in college whose father abandoned his family before he reached his second birthday. It was very seldom he desired to bring his dad up in conversation. As far as he was concerned, his dad was not his dad and the only thing he had in common with the man was DNA. I asked him in what ways he believed his life was affected by the absence of his biological father, for better or for worse.

How much could I know about it? I don't know what it's even like to have a dad, much less realize what I'm missing without one. I never even think about it because it's not a big deal. It was good that he left when he did.

I wasn't shocked by his response. I truly felt that his dad's absence from his life was affecting him in some way, whether he was aware of it or not. Just because it was a long time ago doesn't erase the reality that one of his parents did, in fact, leave him and the rest of his family behind. Even if they left years ago, the truth still holds that they are not in the here and the now. I really pushed him to try to uncover any struggles and areas in his life that may have been rooted in the absence of his father.

Just a few days after that conversation, we were at lunch. He told me after spending some time praying and really asking the Lord to turn over stones in his past and in his heart, he discovered deep anger and bitterness toward his dad and his family situation in general. He was broken. He admitted how it hurt not having those experiences that normal children have with a father. He said it hurt that he never got to go camping.

He never got to go fishing.

He didn't know how to change his oil.

He didn't know how to check his tires.

He was lacking so much in a father-taught world.

He admitted that it hurt knowing and having to comprehend that he was left behind.

For those in these very same circumstances, we understand that real moms and real dads exist. We just struggle to know what it's like to actually have ones of our own, ones that stay around and ones that care.

Best-selling author Donald Miller expresses similar thoughts in his book *Father Fiction*:

For me a father is nothing more than a character in a fairy tale. And I know fathers are not like dragons in that fathers actually exist, but I don't remember feeling that a father existed for me. I know they are real people. I have seen them on television, sliding their arms around their women in grocery stores, and I have seen them in the malls and in the coffee shops, but these were characters in other people's stories, and I never stopped to question why one of these characters wasn't living in our house. I don't say this out of self-pity, because in a way I don't miss having a father any more than I miss having a dragon. But in another way, I find myself wondering if I missed out on something important.5

For countless children, this decision that was expressed to us as being "for our good" doesn't feel very good. It doesn't feel very good at all. We feel that we are missing out on something important. Why is it that our lives seem to have been made worse by this? We are now in situations where we are made fun of, singled out, cast aside. We feel abnormal and different.

Because it's different when you get back home from traveling over the holidays and you and your brother and sister go over to your dad's apartment and you get a few gifts.

That's not the same.

That's not Christmas.

When I was little and didn't understand any of it I thought it was neat getting two sets of presents, and then on my birthday, getting two parties and two sets of cards and two cakes.

But beneath all of the wrapping paper and candles and Christmas trees, there is a hole.

There's space.

There's a hole that causes you to wish things had turned out differently because, when it's all swept away, the parties, the clothes, the toys, and the family trips, none of it seems to matter. Gifts fade away. Barbies and Legos get put in the garage and sold. Children grow up and, when they do, they're not going to be concerned with the Playstations, the playhouses, and the action figures they got when they were twelve. They're going to wonder where their parents went and if, before they left, they did everything they could to find a way to stay.

They're going to wonder if their dad really believed a new bike would make up for the large space in the bed next to their mom where he used to sleep. They're going to question whether or not their mom thought buying them a new car would make them forget about the empty space in the driveway where she used to park.

Gifts and things that have a price tag aren't parents.

Parents are present.

Parents give hugs.

Parents help you with your homework.

Parents make you feel better when you're sick.

Parents tell you everything is going to be okay.

Parents are around.

Parents are there.

And when they are, you're able to throw away that old box of cereal.

L|2

• • • • •

CHAPTER TWO
AFRAID

The floor was never comfortable.

It was hard and cold, and the blankets were scratchy. Some of them felt more like sandpaper than they did cotton bed linens. I never could get situated. I'd toss, and I'd turn. I'd take the covers off and put them back on. Using a blanket to make a sleeping bag really just doesn't work the same as a normal sleeping bag. It'd take hours to fall asleep sometimes. I would just lie there and stare at the ceiling, or at least in the direction of the ceiling. It was too dark to really see anything. Sometimes I'd find myself staring under the bed, hoping and praying something didn't come out from under there and eat me.

I'd think about getting up and going back upstairs to my bed. It would be so much more comfortable. I'd be warm and my sheets would be soft instead of feeling like something from Home Depot.

But I stayed.

I always stayed.

I stayed because I knew I was safe. I stayed because, even though I couldn't get comfortable, I wasn't anxious or nervous. I could lie there and know that rescue was an arm's reach away in the bed above me. No matter what the nightmare was that brought me downstairs to my make-shift bed, it was erased and forgotten there on the cold floor next to my two protectors. It wasn't the same upstairs. It felt like they were miles away. It would take too long for me to get to them if something happened. It didn't matter that my brother was sleeping directly above me on the top bunk and it didn't give me comfort that my sister was in the room next to mine.

Because it's different with mommy and daddy.

It's different when you know they are near. It's different when you can see your dad's hand hanging off the edge of the bed from just inches above. No harm can reach you. Their presence emits a protective force field, shielding off any incoming danger. And their room was safe. I remember nights where the dream was too vivid and too scary, and I'd travel down the stairs and crawl up in bed with them and drift off to sleep while their arms wrapped around me. Nothing could penetrate those arms. I was locked in. No blanket in the world could do what their arms could.

Having them there and knowing that all was well inside our home was its own form of protection. It was knowing that when I got home from school they would be there soon after. I'd stay outside in the driveway or in the yard just to see their two cars pull in. Some days mom would be first and some days dad's little blue Civic would be the first to make the turn onto our street. When those two cars were parked, all was well.

Having them there let me breathe. Having dad inside, sitting in his blue leather chair watching the news, while taking in a few Coors Lights, gave comfort. Seeing mom in the kitchen through the window from outside in the driveway gave me confidence. It meant that I could smile and play basketball with reckless abandon like any other carefree kid. It gave me assurance in our home. It provided security. Knowing they were inside allowed me to trust that our home was safe and that once inside the door tension released. All discomfort and fear and insecurity and unrest vanished. It didn't matter what happened at school or who said what. It didn't matter if hearts got broken or knees were scraped.

Tears were wiped.

Knees were cleaned.

It's as if life was this giant game of hide-and-seek or tag and home was base.

Because it was home.

There was always somewhere to go and knowing there is always somewhere to go to be safe means something to a kid. It changes things when you know that there is a place of refuge. It makes you feel good and it makes the bad things that happen seem not as bad. Because home is there when you get in a fight. Home is there when you fail a test. Home is there when you get dumped. Home is there when you don't make the team.

Home is always there when everything in your world seems to be shattering into tiny pieces, all at the same time.

Because it's home.

Until it's not anymore.

WALLS

There's this wall at my grandma's house. The same house where I met Buzz Lightyear for the first time and understood what it took to erect an underwater metropolis.

It's been standing since the 1960s. Ever since I can remember, my brother and sister and I have been climbing and walking that wall. We'd see who could make it around the entire thing without falling off. It's about as wide as the length of a single red brick. It slopes in places and bends in others. Most of the navigation was easy except for a few key spots where some brush from the woods had grown over. Those spots were always the most difficult. Most of the time you'd climb down, unscathed, the same as when you started. Other times you may leave the brick road with pricks and pokes from briars and sharp branches. Jumping off you felt like you'd die as soon as you hit the ground. We felt so high. It's funny how distance is skewed when you're little. Maybe it's because you want to be more of a daredevil than you actually are. Sadly, in reality my grandma's wall was maybe only five feet high at its highest point. But we still felt dangerous. We still felt brave. We felt like conquerors.

There are countless pictures of us on top of that wall. Poses with friends and cousins. Poses in summer and in winter and fall and spring. We spent our childhood on top of it. It was immensely entertaining for us. And still is.

But entertaining is really all this wall does. That and showing a distinction between whose property is whose. This wall doesn't keep anything out or keep anything in. It's just there.

This wall hasn't and doesn't keep my grandma's house safer and it doesn't protect it from any kind of danger. If anything, it added danger, due to children and grandchildren treating it like a jungle gym!

This wall at my grandma's house wasn't like most walls.

Most walls are built for protection. Most walls keep certain things in and certain things out. It's because that's what walls do. That's why people build them.

And that's why people rebuild them.

There's a story in the Old Testament about the rebuilding of a wall. It's the wall surrounding the city of Jerusalem and the story takes place in the book of Nehemiah.6

In the very beginning of Nehemiah's account we find out the bad news: Jerusalem is unprotected. The city's gates and wall have been destroyed. This is a big problem for the people of the city. These gates and this wall were their security system. This was the city's protection. Now, they are no longer safe. They are exposed. They are defenseless.

Jerusalem is in great trouble.

Jerusalem is in great trouble because this wall was a lot taller than five feet and this wall wasn't built for the amusement of the city's children.

This wall was built for the city's safety.

Because this wall did keep things out and this wall protected Jerusalem from any threat of danger to the people living within the city. This wall insured their defense. Now that this wall has fallen, the city is unsafe. Homes aren't as safe and businesses aren't as protected. People are frantically running around and fearing an attack that could happen at any moment. They're scared because if an attack did come, there is no defense.

Jerusalem is unprotected.

I don't know what it's like to live in a city where the walls fall and an entire population is in danger from enemy attack. I don't know what that feels like. I can't even imagine it.

But I do know what it's like to feel defenseless.

I know what it's like to be afraid and to feel completely exposed and in danger.

I know what it's like to have protection taken away in an instant because that's what happened when he drove away. When my dad left, I cried and I hurt and I ached. Yes, there was emptiness to deal with and confusion to wrestle with but there was just as much fear. I was scared. My safe zone, my place of comfort, my haven, my fortress, my home - it cracked and the walls came down.

And when that happens, it feels as if there is nowhere to go. My house was my last bastion of safety. It was my safety net. And now, what was I supposed to do? I thought my dad was the family's rock and protector. I thought he would always keep us safe and defend us. What was going to happen now? Who was going to keep us safe?

I was so afraid.

I was afraid during the day and all through the night. Home didn't feel like home to me. It felt like someone else's house. It didn't feel like we lived there. I couldn't sleep because I couldn't help but think that someone was going to come and get us. I thought we would be taken. Anybody could come in and harm our family. I'd get in my bunk bed wondering if that night would be the night someone came. I wanted dad to come in and rub my back and to tell me that we were safe. I wanted him to tell me that he would be downstairs. But to me it seemed that the whole world knew that he was gone and so now was the best chance to break in.

I remember thinking that there was a newsletter sent around to all criminals that listed off the best houses to rob, the houses that were the least protected.

And for me, I believed our little house with just our green Dodge Caravan in the driveway to be at the top of that list.

It felt like the front door never shut once he walked out. It was open. We were at risk. We were on display, free for the taking, and he didn't care. Didn't he want us to be protected? What was better than that? What was better than taking care of us? What was better than keeping us safe?

Feeling defenseless made me miss all the yelling and all the fighting. I wanted him to yell at me again. I wanted him and mom to keep fighting. I wanted to be upstairs again with Stu and Grace Anne, with our doors shut and trying to ignore the noise downstairs. I wanted mom to sleep upstairs again and to have him downstairs by himself in their room.

It didn't matter that I was afraid when he got home. It didn't matter that some days after school I'd go with my sister to my aunt's house to stay until we knew both mom and dad were home. It didn't matter that I'd get sick to my stomach if my teachers ever told me that they were going to make a phone call to my parents. Because during those months it was a different kind of fear. I knew at the end of the night, when the yelling stopped and the anger subsided and he went to bed, he went to bed downstairs in his bedroom.

And it didn't matter how afraid I was because I knew after he was done yelling he'd still be there. It was all his anger and his frustration that gave me a sense of comfort because I knew that if anyone ever broke into our house, his temper and his force would be waiting for them.

But when he left, even though our home was a lot quieter and we spoke to each other in calmer voices, I was uneasy. I just wanted him home, even if that meant things going back to how they were when I couldn't do anything right in his eyes and when he cut up Stu's license with a pair of scissors right in front of him because he got in a wreck.

Because now he wasn't there at all and I was afraid.

Recently, over coffee, I spoke with a college student who told me about a conversation he had with one of his co-workers. This co-worker had recently left her husband and moved out of the house into an apartment with her young daughter. When this student asked how the daughter was doing with all the transitions, the woman replied:

She's doing fine. The only thing I haven't understood is that her stomach has been upset and hurting the past couple weeks since we moved.

Everything in this little girl's world just changed. Yes, her stomach has been hurting. Yes, she doesn't feel well. Her family was just broken into two pieces. She was just taken away from her father. He's not down the hall anymore. She's struggling. Her tummy hurts because she's in a brand new environment. A brand new apartment. A brand new room. A brand new family.

For her, a brand new home.

When my friend told me this, my heart broke for this little girl because years ago I was her. Years ago my mom was talking about me at coffee with somebody. Years ago my stomach hurt, and I didn't like adapting to the forced changes going on within my world and within my family.

My guard was up all the time.

I couldn't sleep because home wasn't restful. I couldn't laugh because home wasn't funny. Home was stressful and tense. There was nothing there that untied the knots that were constantly wrapped around my stomach. This is why, when I was outside of the house, I wanted humor in every possible situation, even the serious ones. I wanted to laugh. I *needed* to laugh. And I wanted to see other people laugh. This didn't happen at home and so these places were my only shot. School. Church. Counseling. Baseball practice. Basketball practice. I wanted to feel like a kid. I wanted to make fun of things and tell jokes. I wanted the serious moments to be funny because that's what I desperately wanted to do with everything going on at home.

I was tired of being serious.

I was tired of crying.

I was tired of being on edge.

I was tired of being on the defensive.

I was tired of being afraid.

I was tired of being tired.

Life hurt, and life was scary.

Especially that one night.

I was already in my pajamas. I was in bed, wrapped up in my *101 Dalmatians* sheets while Stu was busy doing some kind of homework on the floor in our bedroom as he always did. He'd take occasional mental breaks to get back into his NBA Live Super Nintendo match up with the Orlando Magic. Grace Anne was in her room watching TV or talking on her see-through, neon phone. It was a normal night.

All of this wasn't anything out of the ordinary.

But then mom said to get downstairs.

I had no idea what was going on. I was fading in and out, drifting off to sleep in bed. Nothing in me wanted to get out from underneath the covers and walk the long trek down the stairs to see what was going on.

But this was urgent.

I wondered if someone tried to break in and mom was getting us out of the house to be safe. That thought paralyzed me. I was in my pajamas. Where would we go? What about Stu's homework? Didn't he need to finish it? We couldn't just leave.

When we got downstairs mom said to get our shoes. At this point, one of my previous thoughts was right: she was getting us somewhere safe. But safe from what?

That's where it all changed. It wasn't because a burglar tried to get in our house or because there was a fire or because our power was out. It was because dad was on his way to the house.

And he was very angry.

It was because mom just got off the phone with him and said he was on his way and she did not know what would happen once he got there.

So we left.

Huddled together with my mom and brother and sister with me in my pajamas, we made the journey through our front yard over to our neighbors to wait and to watch. I was beyond confused. Why was he so mad? What was he coming to do? We peered through the closed blinds from our neighbor's living room. We cut off all the lights and all kids were told to whisper.

We waited.

Soon, his car sped recklessly into the driveway. He got out and went to the door, knocking continuously.

What did he want?

I remember, as it was all happening, thinking it was kind of cool that I got to be at Brandan's late at night. I remember thinking how neat it was that we were getting to hang out on a school night. Looking back, it was a good thing that I was distracted that night. It was a good thing that I couldn't fully process what was going on with my family and why my dad was so upset with my mom. The only thing that wasn't good was that now, for me and my family, it was no longer a burglar that I was afraid of threatening our safety.

It was him.

It was my own dad.

Angry, annoyed, and unsatisfied he peeled out of the driveway and sped off.

This changed everything for me. This changed what I was afraid of and how I slept and how I felt whenever we saw him. Up to this point in my life, even with the yelling and the drinking and all the fights, I never thought my dad would ever hurt me or any of us. The thought never crossed my mind. But now it was different. As time passed, I began to think what would have happened had he not called that night. What if we had been there? What if the door had been unlocked?

After that night in my pajamas it made being at home even more difficult. I'd be outside playing, wondering what would happen if I was alone and he drove up. I didn't like feeling unsafe at my own house and in my own yard. I hated it. I hated it even more that it was my dad that I was afraid of. I knew it wasn't normal and it bothered me. At this point I wanted to be afraid of a burglar again, not him. My aunt would pick me up every Friday from school and take me to Hardee's to get a milkshake and some fries. We did this every week. Some weeks I just wanted to go to her house instead. I'd take a nap on the couch and wait until mom got home. I felt safe there and Aunt Pearl always had this smile on her face that made me feel that things were going to be okay.

But I desperately wanted to feel that way at home.

And moving didn't make things any easier.

We lived in several different apartments and, one summer, even lived with a lady from church. Nothing felt like home because we were there for only a few months. Pack up and then unpack. Then pack up and then unpack again. I didn't like sleeping in a strange place not knowing if I could find the bathroom during the night. I was in someone else's house and in someone else's room. How was I supposed to find mom in the middle of the night if I needed to?

Each time we moved, there was none of his stuff. We didn't have dad stuff. I always wondered if the neighbors noticed. Did they realize it was just four of us? Did they notice there was only one car? Moving into a new neighborhood and a new apartment complex wasn't easy for me. It let everyone know our dad wasn't with us. Maybe some people thought he just wasn't there that day. Maybe he was out of town while we were moving in. Or maybe he was sick in the hospital. Whatever the speculation, we were the ones who knew he wasn't out of town and he wasn't sick.

He just wasn't moving in.

And ever since we started moving into houses and apartments without his stuff it's always been a battle to feel safe. It's always been a struggle to have no fear at night when I am home by myself. As time passes it's reassuring that those nights get fewer and fewer. But every now and then, the eight year-old comes out and wonders about the noise outside my window or the weird sound in the kitchen or if I locked the door or not and if someone can get in easily. I wonder if I left a window open, even if I never opened the windows that day. I wonder if I leave a lot of lights on, will people think I haven't gone to sleep yet and it'd be a bad time to try and steal something?

Because the little boy in me will always want to feel protected and to feel safe. The little boy in me will never like the idea of being on his own. The little boy in me will always want his dad to rise up and beat up the bad guy.

It's tough. As the years pass, you feel that you should stop being scared of things that bothered you when you were a kid. You start to feel that it's time that you should be able to defend yourself and your family. You feel that, if someone came into your house, then you should be able to do what needed to be done to keep your wife and your children safe. But you worry about that happening. You're afraid of that happening.

Because even grown-ups get scared sometimes.

Even grown-ups miss their dads.

Because even 22 years after trying to go to sleep for the first time without him

LEFT

under the same roof, I still have trouble getting to sleep some nights.

L|3

•••• •

CHAPTER THREE
LUNCHES

They were girls' shoes.

Girls' softball cleats.

And I didn't want to wear them. It didn't matter to me that, from the outside and from the design of the shoe, you didn't know if they were girls' shoes or guys' shoes or shoes for softball or baseball or soccer or rugby. None of that mattered to me. What mattered was that I knew my sister used these shoes last year for softball. What mattered was that they were hers. What mattered was that I was wearing my sister's softball cleats for my baseball season.

And it bothered me.

I just wanted a pair of cleats that were mine. I wanted some high-top cleats like all the other kids on my team. These were low-tops. These were used. These weren't new. These weren't cool looking and didn't look like anything special. These weren't flashy.

These weren't mine.

But I laced them up anyway. It was my only option. There was nothing else for me to do but to suck it up and make it look like I loved my shoes and that I was on the cusp of a new trend. But I didn't love them and I wasn't setting any trends. All the other guys had Nike's and Mizuno's. These were Reebok's. Nobody on my team was rocking any low cut Reebok cleats.

Nobody on my team was wearing girls' softball cleats.

But these low-cut cleats from my sister's previous junior high softball season were all I had.

They were all my family could afford.

Mom didn't have the money to get us new shoes each season and sometimes that meant sharing. It's because she had three grown kids living and eating and breathing and drinking and sleeping in our apartment while she, with her reception job, was pulling in $20,000. And that wasn't enough to squeeze in new cleats every season for each of us while, at the same time, making sure dinner was on the table and socks were on our feet and clothes were on our backs. But it wasn't just new cleats. This meant no soccer shorts or basketball shoes or shin guards or jerseys or hats or gloves or bats. Not from her bank account anyway.

This made me jealous as a little kid.

I was jealous when I looked at everybody else and everything they had. Everyone at practice had the fitted hats and the belts and the special pants. I wanted those things. I wanted more than the standard white pants with the elastic waist and the cardboard looking hat that no matter how tight I snapped it still looked eight sizes too big for my tiny head.

I wanted the fitted hat and the grey pants with the belt loops.

I wanted the super huge bat bag that clipped on the fence in the dugout and that had room for a helmet and a small person.

And I wanted to be the kid with the really cool dad.

I remember in little league when my friends' dads would come and help out at practice coaching first and third base during the games. I remember them buying stuff for our team and bringing pitching machines to practice and helping us with our swings. Then during basketball season, they came to the gym to help us with our jump shots and rebounding and dribbling. In all of that I wanted my dad there. I wanted him to help me and to help with my team and to be in the team picture at the end of the season. I've been to so many weddings where, at the rehearsal dinner the night before, the couple played an emotional slideshow filled with childhood pictures. In each one there was always a picture of the groom, on his baseball team when he was little, with his dad standing behind his team. I wanted that. I wanted to be the kid that gave stuff to the team and whose dad was the coolest. I wanted my dad to be the cool coach and to get me cool batting gloves and socks. I wanted him to surprise me with a big pack of Big League Chew at my games that I could share with the other guys.

But he wasn't there and I was getting picked up from and taken to practice by one aunt and getting all the things I needed to make sure I was able to play by another aunt. And neither of them played baseball or basketball. They couldn't come out to practice and help us with our technique and give us hints on our strategy for our next game.

But they stepped in. They filled a need that our family had. They filled a need that I had. They surrounded us and walked through the wreckage from the tornado that hit our home when dad left and, in one fell swoop, left me in pieces.

But in the midst of all that happened and everything that went on in those years after, we were taken care of.

We were provided for.

At night we had beds and in the winter we had heat in our home. When it was cold outside and the weather was harsh, we had a roof over our heads and we were all curled up nice and warm in our sheets on our mattresses.

But I was in a sleeping bag.

Not sheets.

And right near the very bottom of my green sleeping bag near my feet it had been stamped.

This stamp meant something. This stamp told me something.

It told me that this sleeping bag wasn't purchased from Dick's Sporting Goods or Bass Pro Shops. It told me, very simply but very clearly, that this sleeping bag wasn't purchased at all.

This stamp, no bigger than two square inches, told me that this sleeping bag was given. It told me that this sleeping bag was earned. And this tiny emblem told me that this sleeping bag had done a lot more than overnight camping in the mountains and best friend sleepovers in the back yard in the fall.

Property of the U.S. Army.

This sleeping bag was important. It had a story. And it had been all over the world by the time it made it on top of my bed. I slept in this sleeping bag for over a year and never changed my sheets. Because not only was this sleeping bag important, it was important to me. Sure, it kept me warm and some nights a little too toasty. But it wasn't just about the quality of the insulation. That wasn't where the value in this bag was.

It was because my aunt gave me that sleeping bag. And I loved it.

But I loved her more.

You see, when she didn't pick up the phone and hear us scream *Aunt B!* and when she didn't get letters in the mail addressed to *Aunt B!* and when she wasn't running after us on the grassy lawn of Washington D.C. in front of the Capitol building with a fanny-pack around her waist and shorts that looked like they were made out of an American flag, she was in uniform.

And the uniform didn't say *Aunt B!*

It said

Colonel Barbara Jean Smith

Because my aunt was a big deal in the army. In the book, *A Contemporary History of the U.S. Army Nurse Corps,* there's an entire chapter written about her leadership and all of her responsibilities during Operation Desert Storm and Operation Desert Shield.

Chapter 18.

Starting on page 425.

My aunt did great things for our country. But all those things in that book, and everything she accomplished in her 30 years as an Army nurse, don't compare to the ways in which she served my family and served her little sister, my mom. Those tasks and those methods of leadership during Desert Storm are minimal and insignificant to me. They don't compare to how she stepped in and provided leadership and support to our family in our darkest of times when we needed so much.

Because it wasn't just a sleeping bag that she used in Saudi that she gave.

It was shorts and socks and shirts and shoes and shin guards.

It was jerseys and jackets and Jordan's.

It was bats and bags and boots and balls.

It was gloves and gear.

She jumped in and bore part of the weight bearing down on mom's tiny little shoulders. She planted her feet beside mom and put on her helmet and her government issued fatigues and went to war for us. And for Aunt B, while her fighting days were over for her country, her fighting days for our family, her sister and her niece and nephews, were just beginning.

When I look back to these times I don't know where my family would be without her. I really don't. And sure, there was stuff that she provided for us and helped us with, but it was the continual emotional support of knowing she was there. It was her constant love and care and provision. Knowing she was on the other end of the phone talking with mom and giving mom comfort and encouragement and strength when she needed it.

It wasn't just about Aunt B coming in, and for all those years, buying our shoes and our jerseys and our socks and our bat bags and our gloves and our running shorts and our track spikes. Because even though she did all that, it was giving mom confidence and telling her we'd make it through that truly comforted us. It was her being there, right next to us in the trenches. It was knowing she was a phone call away. Because there were certainly times we didn't know if we would make it. Right when dad left mom was an assistant kindergarten teacher at my elementary school.

She was making $11,500 a year.

And that had to cover things that it just couldn't cover. We had to move out, get a moving truck, and find an apartment. That summer in 1997 was the summer we stayed with a woman from church. And even though the house creeped me out and even though it was weird staying with a lady that I didn't know that well, knowing that she knew why we were there, it was what we needed. It was all we had at the time and it was a blessing.

And even in that summer when all our ends had to be met with $11,500, we were provided for. But it was hard knowing that much of the provision and care wasn't coming from dad. It was coming from a collection of sources. Sources that weren't him and sources that made us realize this was the way it was going to be from now on.

Just a few months ago a friend told me how his dad, who had walked out on his mom years before, decided he wasn't going to be helping out with his tuition anymore. He pulled the plug and, while my friend already had a job, it was forcing his mom to take up another job to help with what wasn't being covered. With tears welling up in his eyes, he told me

If my dad knows what this is doing to my mom and me, why is he doing this? Aren't I his son?

It's not easy processing things and understanding why our parents leave and why, it seems, they don't want to care for us anymore. It's hard and it makes us sad.

It changes so many things and so many aspects of our lives. It changes the big things and it changes even the little things.

Because after my dad left, lunches for school just weren't the same that next semester.

I remember how I felt every day at school with my little brown bag lunch. That little brown bag reminded me that he wasn't at home and that he wasn't helping mom with the groceries anymore.

Because lunches were different.

Lunches were smaller.

BROWN BAGS

I had no idea what it was.

The only thing I knew was that it looked too gross to be a wedding gift. I thought it might be a joke.

What in the world could it be? It looked like mud scraped up from the ground and thrown into a rubber container that was then placed in the freezer.

Seriously, what is this?

And then it hit me. It was a container full of cookie dough. But not just any cookie dough. It was homemade chocolate chip cookie dough. But not just any homemade chocolate chip cookie dough.

It was Brenda's homemade chocolate chip cookie dough.

This cookie dough represented more than the warm, moist cookies it would soon transform into in the oven. This cookie dough represented school lunches since I was 12 years-old. This cookie dough reminded me of the hundreds of lunches that Kathryn and I had together from 6th grade until we graduated high school.

Because for seven years I stole bites from the cookies Brenda packed in Kathryn's lunch.

And they were always delicious. Brenda's baking was never disappointing and it always made me a lunch thief.

There would even be days when Brenda would send me my own cookie. And after all those years, here we were at my wedding, and right in front of me was a container full of that cookie dough.

The truth is, it wasn't just the cookies. It was everything in Kathryn's lunch box that looked delicious and appealing. I wanted everything. And it wasn't just hers. It was Nick's, too.

And Hatcher's.

And Maggie's.

And Meredith's.

And Adam's.

It was because mom just didn't have the time in the morning to make us elaborate lunches. She was too busy with three kids trying to get us out the door and to the bus stop before she headed to work. It's because she didn't have time when she got home late in the evening to make cookies. And it's because we didn't have the money at the grocery store to get anything outside of what was necessary. It's because our grocery list wasn't that long.

It couldn't be.

But Kathryn and Nick would sit down at lunch on our round circle seats and open what was, to me, two very large treasure chests. I never knew what would be inside. There honestly were days when I'd think about their lunches in class, wondering what Brenda and Nancy packed for them that day. A close third was always Hatcher's. His mom would make these homemade cheddar saltine crackers that were absolutely amazing. It was always a good day if those crackers made their way into Hatcher's lunchbox.

There was always so much to see. Sandwiches with lettuce and tomato and all different kinds of meat and chips and crackers and goldfish and beef jerky. I remember the day in 5th grade when Nick brought a Lunchable and it was the little pizzas. I wanted little pizzas.

I looked around at lunch because, when you're 12, you don't know how to process what is happening with the finances when it's only one parent working. You don't understand. You don't know how that changes things. So I was angry that I had to take peanut butter and jelly sandwiches. I never liked the chips mom bought. They were always an off-brand of something else that probably tasted amazing. I always had Whales instead of Goldfish because Goldfish were really expensive. And sometimes we'd get Dr. Thunder instead of Dr. Pepper.

But I wanted Goldfish.

I wanted Dr. Pepper.

Sometimes Nick would bring these pepperoni sandwiches with cheese and mayonnaise on them. It tasted like a pizza in between two pieces of bread. And I loved pepperoni. But pepperoni cost more than peanut butter. They'd top their lunches off with a Coke or a Gatorade or a Capri-Sun or maybe even a Sunny D. All of that beat my Gatorade bottle, with the wrapper stripped off, filled with water.

I was embarrassed.

I felt like my lunch showed everyone what was happening at home. It made me feel like they knew we didn't have a lot of money and that things were super tight. Lunches made me think everyone knew that my lunch was the lunch of a kid who only had one parent at home.

Four little items, maybe five some days, adding an oatmeal raisin pie or a Little Debbie cake, tucked in a little brown paper bag. My name was on it to keep us from grabbing the wrong lunch at home on our way out the door.

But I didn't like the bag.

I wanted a lunchbox. And not just any lunchbox.

I dreamed of getting a blue Arctic Zone lunchbox.

I felt like everyone at the table had an Arctic Zone lunchbox.

Blue. Pink. Red. Green.

And they all came with little containers for each lunch item. Everyone's lunches were so high-tech. And even the ones that didn't have the containers had cool bags.

I remember wanting my sandwich and chips to be in Zip-loc bags.

Zip-loc bags with the little finger with the smiley face on the box.

But Zip-loc bags weren't as cheap as the store brand bags that you tucked one side into the other and wrapped up.

Things were just different when it came to the grocery store and what we needed for the apartment and what we had for dinner and what mom put in our lunches. It took me awhile to understand it and not get bitter or angry about what we were eating or what I got packed for lunch or what we couldn't do. It didn't make sense to me as a kid. I didn't understand cutting back and not being able to buy Zip-loc bags.

I didn't understand not having money for lunch boxes or pepperonis or Lunchables or cookies or Capri-Suns.

I didn't understand why we were having cereal or toaster strudels for dinner. I didn't want a fried egg for dinner or a grilled cheese or a Pop Tart. I wanted something better. Something different. Something that I knew someone else was having for dinner too. I didn't hear my friends at school talk about the pop tart they had the previous night for dinner or the four bowls of Corn Pops they had.

It's funny thinking back to these days and these nights when I was younger. It's been 18 years and I still get picked on about the things I'll eat for dinner. Throughout college and even in high school, people couldn't believe I hadn't had certain things like homemade dumplings or homemade lasagna or homemade fried chicken. They just didn't get it. I tried telling them that mom just didn't have the time because she was working. We just didn't have the money for certain things that may have seemed normal to other people.

When I got married, my wife asked me what I'd like to eat for dinner throughout the week and I'd suggest cereal.

Because now, I love cereal.

I am used to cereal.

Cereal is dinner food for me.

And looking back, I know that my mom was no less a provider for our family just because we ate cereal for dinner instead of homemade chicken potpie.

Because let's revisit the lunchbox.

Or lunch bag.

I mentioned there were consistently four staple items in my bag, maybe a fifth on special days.

A Gatorade bottle of water without the wrapper.

A peanut butter and jelly sandwich.

A folded, not zipped, bag of chips.

And a note.

My mom wrote me a note every day and put it in my bag. It would either be on a little post-it note shaped like a flower, or a normal square, or she'd write it on the inside of the bag.

Praying for you today, Buddy! Love you more than you know!

And she would put a scripture reference below a little smiley face that she would always draw.

No, my mom couldn't buy me a blue lunchbox or expensive pepperoni slices from the deli or make me homemade pasta or put Scooby snacks in my lunch or use Zip-loc bags. But she was doing other things. She was doing more important things. She was doing far greater things for me than giving me Sunny D instead of Food Lion brand orange juice.

She was providing more for me in those notes than she could have ever done with any amount of money or lettuce or chicken or lasagna. None of that mattered. She gave me more provision and care and love in her 10-15 words on a flower note pad than 1,000 cookies or 2,000 slices of pepperoni could have ever done.

This note made my lunch the best lunch at the entire table and in the entire school.

And I wouldn't trade those notes for any cookie or little pizza or cheddar cracker. And I wouldn't trade my mom for the best cook in the world. Because I don't care if she cooked or not. I don't care if she baked or not. And I don't care how many times before I graduated I had Cap'n Crunch for supper.

She was, and is, the greatest mom and woman I have ever known.

And she provided abundantly for us the things we truly needed.

But the reality was that we couldn't do even what may be normal for many families. We couldn't do dessert every night and BLT's for lunch every day. And those things aren't bad things. It's just that those things couldn't happen because there wasn't enough money to do those things and for bills to get paid. And even then, there were many times when even bills couldn't get paid with what mom was bringing in. That's why we had eggs and cereal and grilled cheese.

I remember mom being so tired when she got home from work. I remember her exhaustion. Even though mom wasn't out in a brickyard breaking rocks or making concrete or building a railroad, it made sense why she was tired. She was carrying the load for us. She was emotionally and physically carrying us through and providing everything she could for us. She was doing it all. And I used to think she was doing it alone ever since dad left but that wasn't true at all.

Because there was always a bill due each month that mom couldn't pay. On paper, mom's paychecks never came close to adding up to what was needed for bills and food and what we needed. For the longest time, I wanted to know how we stayed afloat and how we didn't go into debt and get chased after by bounty hunters and the IRS.

Mom and I spent some time together recently, and she told me what she would do with the bills she knew she just couldn't pay. She told me that sometimes she'd keep them in the mailbox or leave them propped up on the counter. She told she would set the bill down and say

Lord, I can't do it. I can't do it this month. You have to take care of this one.

When hearing this I remember thinking

. . . and?

And for 12 years, mom's payments were on time and always accounted for. Every bill paid. Never a month where we went under. It's here that I realized just how much our church body surrounded our family and carried us through. It's here that I realized just how much our own family surrounded us and took on our burdens. It's here that I realized that while my dad left and his provision for our family faded, the provision of our True Father and Provider came through in ways I had never seen.

I started to think back over the years and all the youth retreats and camps and school trips we went on. Mom couldn't pay for a single one of those. There were three of us and if we all wanted to go that would end up being a lot of money. So how was it that we never missed a trip? How was it that we always got to go and how was it that even sometimes she went with us? Once again, as a testimony to the families and the friends in our church, people provided for us so graciously and generously. I can't tell you the name of one single person who paid my way to the individual camps and retreats throughout my time in the youth at First Baptist. The people were always a mystery. Never wanting credit. Never asking for anything in return.

In February of 1999, a large group of students was headed on a long weekend ski trip to Snowshoe Mountain, West Virginia. I had never been skiing and the trip sounded amazing. Chartered bus. Cold weather. Learn to ski. Snow. Unfortunately, the trip was close to $300 just for the three days. Mom was heartbroken but knew there just wasn't a way that I could go. It just wasn't going to happen. I remember crying in my room. I was so frustrated. I wanted to go.

But just a day before the crew headed north, mom got a call at work from church, and they told her that if I wanted to go, someone had sent in a check for the full amount designated for me to have a spot on the trip. I couldn't believe it. Who knew that I wanted to go? Who would do that?

This one small story is one of hundreds in the mix of how my family was provided for through the years in my dad's absence. No, the Lord didn't plant a money tree in our backyard or show us some treasure chest buried somewhere. But He provided for our needs. And every month there would be a random check from someone at church that maybe we knew or maybe we didn't. There'd be a check from someone in our family sending us a love gift to help because they knew our situation. These things happened all the time. And I never knew just how much of it was going on until recently.

But I do remember mom working so hard and I remember all that she did. Pick us up from practice, take us to prayer breakfast at Hardee's, pick our friends up for school, take them home from games, drive us to our friend's neighborhood.

She was superwoman.

But it wasn't because of her strength and her ability to provide.

It was because of the Father's.

And He did.

Always.

Without fail.

L|4

CHAPTER FOUR
SUNDAYS

It was two o'clock.

In the morning.

That's when the shipment came in. That's when the trucks pulled in the loading dock in the back of the store and started to unload. That's when all the shelves got restocked and the aisles refilled. The store became brand new again. Untouched. Organized. Neat. Uncluttered.

For just a few hours, Yoda was back on the racks, hanging next to Han Solo and Princess Leia and Greedo and a variety of Stormtroopers, along with the other random figurines of characters that no one ever saw in the movie but were confirmed to be in it. It was always those figurines that Target and Walmart and Toys-R-Us had 37 of but not one of the recognizable favorites.

And that was Yoda.

Yoda couldn't be found anywhere. He was the one character that everyone was going after. He was the one figurine everybody wanted. He was the one that people and entire families were searching for.

And he was the one that dads were waiting for at Toys-R-Us at 2AM to see how many showed up on the late night shipment.

My dad loved surprising me at birthdays and Christmas with rare Star Wars figurines and collectibles. Sometimes it wasn't even an occasion. A box would be next to me when I woke up or downstairs at the table or on the couch. And almost more than giving them to me, he loved searching for them and finding them and seeing which stores were getting which figurines at what time. And soon, in just a few years, I had the entire collection and every random character accounted for.

I knew my dad loved Star Wars. I knew he loved the hunting and the finding and the waiting. No matter what it was. Whether it was a movie or a figurine or a polar bear for my sister or a rare collector's card for Stu or a new video game for the Super Nintendo.

It didn't matter.

And he always loved doing whatever it was with us. One Christmas I think my dad spent more time playing my new Star Wars Nintendo 64 game than I did. He sat there, blue and white robe and leather slippers with coffee, all day. I think he beat the game by 5PM, including any secret or bonus levels.

Maybe it was Star Wars.

But maybe it was just video games in general.

I will never forget the time that our town was under a severe tornado warning. We had candles ready and gallons of water ready for eminent destruction. We were prepared for survival.

But it was November of 1994.

And Super Nintendo's Donkey Kong Country had just come out.

My dad and brother jolted off to blockbuster to snag one of the last copies. There in the midst of tornados and hurricane rain and thunder my dad and brother were rushing off to rent a video game. And so that night, as my mom and sister and me huddled off ready for the power to cut out any minute and for the roof to blow off, my dad and brother were off in his room making their way through Tree Top Town and Oil Drum Alley.

All those are such vivid memories of him.

I can remember how he held the controller, and how he'd throw it down on the ground when he died, the game was over, and he'd have to restart. Especially when he played Zelda. He always thought moving the controller farther left or right when he needed his little guy to jump actually helped the guy jump farther and more accurately. Sadly, Xbox Kinect wasn't around in 1994, so moving the controller made no difference.

All these sounds and movements he'd make, they're all things I can hear and picture so easily. They're all small little videos that play over and over in my head with full surround sound and 4K picture quality.

In remembering and looking back, Chuck Swindoll writes,

I am deeply indebted to the man who raised me. Certain smells and sounds now instantly remind me of my dad. Oyster stew. The ocean breeze. Smoke from an expensive cigar. The nostalgic whine of a harmonica. A camping lantern and white gas.7

When I look back, I can't think of being taught anything by my dad that I now carry with me. Sure I can tie my shoes and I can hold a baseball bat and I can use a fork and go to the bathroom. And sure, I can tell you all the random characters' names from every Star Wars film because I had them in bags in my closet. And if you need, I can tell you how to get the secret stars in Super Mario 64. But that's not what Swindoll is talking about. Those aren't things that last and provide necessary foundational beams for growing up and maturing and learning and living.

The writer of Proverbs says that the children of a righteous man will be blessed.8

I know full well the Lord has blessed me and my family abundantly. He has protected and provided for us. He has saved us. He has shown so much grace and mercy. And that's why he blesses, out of sheer mercy and grace because of what Christ has done.

But I didn't learn those things from my dad. I didn't learn about God's ultimate rescue, His plan for the ultimate restoration and the renewal of all things by way of His Son, from the mouth of my father.

Because yes, he loved Yoda and Darth Vader and Donkey Kong and Jason from Power Rangers.

He just didn't love Sundays.

PEWS

He had to switch to chewy lifesavers.

He kept two bags worth in the bottom console in his white '91 Pontiac Trans Sport van. This van reminded you of the Millennium Falcon when you sat in the passenger seat because the dashboard was about six feet deep.

But down in that bottom compartment was lifesaver upon lifesaver upon lifesaver.

Endless colors.

That compartment, now filled with Lifesavers, used to be filled with a wide assortment of Jolly Ranchers. They were dad's favorite candy. He'd pop in one after the other while driving around making his business calls and visiting clients. I never knew why he liked them so much. I hated taking the wrapper off because I never felt like they came off easily. After tossing one back in my mouth, I felt like every time, I'd pull a piece of the wrapper off that was secretly stuck to the candy. I was fond of green apple though.

But he had to switch to chewy lifesavers.

Because there I was, drawing on the church bulletin. I remember his arm was around me and it was as if it was just he and I in a sea of empty pews, all with their red plush cushions.

His arm was around me.

I was drawing.

Bill was preaching.

And dad was crunching.

I remember exactly what I was drawing. Ramses, the North Carolina mascot, draped in a basketball uniform dunking a basketball quite authoritatively.

With his hoof.

It never made sense to me how he was able to hold the ball, but I guess that wasn't the point of the sketch I was drawing from memory. The original image was on one of my brother's tee shirts.

After finishing my ram masterpiece I went on to tracing hair, glasses, faces, dresses, and suits. I always loved drawing and doodling during the service. It protected me from any boredom that might envelop me.

I was nine years-old. My attention span was 45 seconds.

But I didn't know who the people were on the front of our bulletin. Never seen them before. Didn't know if they attended or not. But I did know them quite well from my art sessions every Sunday. I'd rework their hair and give them some new teeth and redesign their fashion choices.

And when I was in the zone I was in the zone.

I couldn't tell you one word Bill preached those Sundays.

But I can tell you everything that happened, second by second, moment by moment, and fear by fear, that Sunday my dad started choking on his grape Jolly Rancher.

He started coughing but I thought nothing of it. But then he kept coughing and it got louder and louder and there started to be a lot more movement. At first I was embarrassed because it was so loud and he just kept going.

But then he got up.

And so did Charlie Choate.

I put down my 3" yellow pencil and looked over, but Mrs. Thompson quickly used her hand to turn my chin.

Don't you look over there, sweetie. Don't you look over there.

I heard some adult down the row whisper that his face was purple. There my dad was, in the far right aisle of the sanctuary, losing his life by way of a tiny little Jolly Rancher.

My dad was going to die in church.

And Bill kept preaching.

I was so mad at Bill that day. I remember wanting to stand up and yell

He's choking! Can't you see he is choking! Stop preaching and do something! Stop preaching and help him!

But he didn't.

And after what seemed to me like 30 minutes of Mr. Choate with his thick arms giving my dad the Heimlich and making all this noise, out popped the candy and in went air back into my dad's lungs.

Charlie Choate saved my dad's life that day, right in the far right aisle of the old sanctuary of First Baptist Church. Funny thing is, that building isn't even standing anymore. It was knocked down several years later and we all moved into the new sanctuary across the field. It had green pews and green carpet. All that's left of that old sanctuary resides in memories; memories and the two stained-glass windows that were preserved and placed in the new building.

And it's not just that old sanctuary with red pew cushions and red carpet that can now only be accessed through memories.

It's my dad sitting in a pew, old or new, beside me and with our family as well.

Because dad didn't come to church much.

That memory of him choking is the only Sunday I can remember him sitting in the pew with us, even though I know he came more than that one day. But all I can remember is that one Sunday.

I know it was more than that one time because I remember being in the woods on that special occasion.

I remember him wearing his red Chicago Bulls shirt.

I remember the street we were on and I remember we parked right in front my 5th grade girlfriend's house.

Jennifer.

We parked and went walking through the woods that day because mom and dad decided they were getting back together. We were going to be a family again. We were going to live together again and dad was going to be in our house again and we were going to have movie nights together again and he was going to be under the same roof sleeping again.

I would get to see him shave and get ready for work and read the paper while he had his coffee and ate his breakfast.

Life was returning to the way it was.

But here in the woods we placed a piece of wood shaped like a tombstone. It had dad's name on it and it had the date. Because here in the woods we were burying things.

We buried his old life.

We buried his old way of doing things.

We buried what was the past.

We buried because dad's old life was over and his new life had begun.

Mom desperately wanted dad to lead our family in this way. She wanted him to pursue Christ and lead his children in that. She wanted him to lead her to treasure Christ above all things and to be a godly husband and a godly father. These things she told him before they agreed to begin their marriage again.

And so he returned home.

And he returned, for a time, to sitting in the pew with us.

But I can't remember much when he started coming back to church. I can't remember any of our Sunday morning routines where I'd come downstairs and get in bed with him while he watched TV and read the cartoons. I can't remember him with his coffee while mom was in the bathroom getting ready.

I can't remember us all hopping in the car together and making the drive downtown and parking and walking into church as a family.

I can't remember.

All those things are things that I know happened and things that I know we did together. I know he was there and I know sometimes he'd even take up the offering in church. I just can't visualize any of it. I can't access those images and those snippets of memory.

Similarly, I can't remember him reading my Bible with me or doing family devotions or praying with me before bed or telling me why everything in the Bible was so important and why we went to church.

But these things, unlike the previous list, are because my dad didn't do them. It's not because they're memories that exist and I just can't access them. It's because they didn't happen. It's because teaching my brother and my sister and my mom and me to treasure Jesus above all else wasn't something my dad did and it wasn't something he passed on to us. My dad didn't teach me how to be a godly man and he didn't teach me how to be a godly husband.

My dad taught me about Star Wars and UNC sports. He taught my brother about collectors' cards and math and video games. And that's what we have. That's what got passed on and those are the things we have from childhood. When I gave all my Star Wars figurines away, they weren't toys to me. They were years of memories and hours of waiting at Toys-R-Us. If you asked me what was valuable to my dad, I would say those things. Those were the things that we understood to be important to him.

For my brother, it's that bookshelf.

The Scriptures instruct us a bit differently. The writer of Deuteronomy says that we must love the Lord with everything we have.9 It says that He should be above everything else in our lives. And it tells us to teach that diligently to our children and to talk about the Lord with them and to tell them all that He has done when we are at home. To talk about Him when we are at dinner and when we go outside in the backyard and focus on Him when we are going to bed and have Him in our minds when we are waking up. We are to think about these things.

The writer says to put them all over your house.

Remember and teach all that the Lord has done.

Remember and teach to love Him above all things.

More than Star Wars.

More than video games.

More than baseball.

More than running.

More than polar bears.

More than cars.

More than jobs.

More than money.

More than houses.

More than families.

He goes on to say that when your children ask you what the Scriptures mean and why God has commanded the things He has, tell them.10 Tell them about God's rescue and His work of restoration. Tell them all that God has done to bring us to Himself. Tell them that God has commanded these things for our good, not for our destruction.

But I didn't ask my dad because I knew my dad didn't have the answers.

And I knew it didn't bother him that he didn't.

Because when dad got back in the driver's seat and was the one taking us to church and when he returned to the pew, he wasn't there for long. It wasn't long before things drifted back to the way they were. He stopped coming. He stopped driving. He stopped getting out of bed before we left for Sunday school.

He stopped.

But what about the tombstone?

What about the woods?

What about all those things you said and the things you promised us? What about the things you said would be different? What about all the things you said about wanting to go to church and wanting to live differently? What about loving Jesus and wanting that to be a part of your life and our family and a part of how you fathered us?

What about all those things?

They weren't real.

They were lies.

He didn't want to teach us. He didn't want to tell us about God's mighty hand with Jonah or David or Solomon or Jonathan. He didn't want to tell us about Zacchaeus or Jacob or Nehemiah or Noah.

He didn't want to tell us about Joseph or Mary.

Or their baby that came.

He didn't care to tell us about their Son, Jesus.

But the Psalmist says parents must teach the things they have heard and known about the Lord and not hide the truth from their children.11 To teach the glorious deeds of the Lord and His might and all that He has done to children so that they may know of the wonderful truths and that their children may know it and their children's children.

Teach them these things so that they may hope in the Lord and not forget Him.

In the past few years, the Barna Group, a research group based in California, published findings that showed the main problem for young people dropping out and leaving the church and their faith is a faith development issue.12 David Kinnaman, in his book *You Lost Me: Why Young Christians Are Leaving Church... And Rethinking Faith*, says it's a disciple-making problem. He says the church is not adequately preparing the next generation to follow Christ faithfully.

This includes families. Children struggle to treasure Christ and to follow Him because they don't see their parents doing this. Christ isn't the most important thing to them. Christ isn't what gets passed on.

It's Wheaties boxes and Jabba the Hut.

I wanted my dad in church with us. I wanted him to pray with me before bed. I wanted him to teach me the Bible. And I wanted to see him reading his Bible. I wanted to see him praying in the morning. I wanted to see him serving mom and doing things for her. I wanted my dad to show me what a godly man was and how a godly man acted and what a godly man did.

I wanted my dad to be a godly father.

But he wasn't.

And he didn't even want to be.

I remember my dad sending me an email one day after I had asked him something about church, him going, or why he didn't want to go.

Son, let's get something straight. The Christian home you grew up in was your mother's doing, not mine.

That was his email.

And while it breaks my heart to know that about my dad, I remain and will forever remain grateful for the dedication my mom had of keeping us in church and of always focusing our attention on Jesus. Jesus is what my mom passed on to us without a doubt. She passed on how life looks and feels and moves when you are wrapped up in Him and love Him more than anything. To not just believe in Him, but to believe Him wholeheartedly. Some days it felt like too much and I felt like she was too preachy, like she was forcing something on us that we didn't want at the time. But I came to learn that's not what my mom was doing.

She wasn't imposing.

She wasn't indoctrinating.

She was investing.

My mom planted daily seeds in our lives that have later harvested much fruit that sustains us in our lives. That fruit was planted by seeds of Truth and it's that kind of impact and investment that lasts.

Luke Skywalker's leg will fall off and the detailed painting will get scraped.

But Jesus will last.

Jesus will endure.

And Jesus will stand strong when families and father-son relationships crumble and when bank accounts go red.

Jesus will remain when athletic ability disappears and hometown notoriety fades.

It's because Jesus is the one Treasure and the one family heirloom that will never get sold or put in the attic.

And He alone is the one thing above all else that children must learn from parents.

Yes, as children we need our parents to teach us how to tie our shoes. We need them to teach us how to play catch. We need them to teach us how to brush our teeth and how to hold a pencil. We need them to teach us how to use a fork. We need them to teach us how to change our oil, how to put on makeup, how to do our homework, how to paint our nails. We need them to teach us the little things.

But more than anything, children need for parents to teach the bigger things—the things that will matter the most when everything else loses its value. As children, we need our parents to teach us the most important thing:

The truth of the saving work of the life, death, and resurrection of Jesus.

We need the truth of Christ planted in the hearts of the next generation.

Our hearts.

Our generation.

It is this one thing that is of utmost importance.

C. S. Lewis says to put the first things first and the second things get thrown in.

However, if you put the second things first then you lose them both.13

It can't just be on Sundays or Saturday nights or whenever church is. That won't make a difference and it won't make an impression. Family counselor and speaker, Dr. Bob Barnes, says that as parents the goal is to raise up godly adults. He says this takes more than one day a week. He explains it by using the image of wearing a pair of glasses. After months and years, an impression, an indentation, on the nose where the glasses sit day after day, begins to get more and more defined and more and more visible. Barnes says this is the way it is with parenting and teaching Christ to children.

It takes time.

It takes years, not just days.

It takes daily consistency and daily saturation, not just one day every week for a few hours.

Parents must know how significant sharing the truth of the gospel with their children is. This is the truth children need. These are the lessons we need to hear. These are the steel beams we need laid early on to build our lives upon. Right now children are losing the truth of the gospel message and the consequences of this are incredibly dangerous.

They are eternally significant.

We need homes that are saturated with an abundant love for the Son and hope in His sacrifice. We need homes that proclaim the promises of Luke's gospel, that because of the Jesus' resurrection, forgiveness of sins through repentance is available. We need homes that show us how precious and priceless Jesus is. We need our parents to pass on this treasure to us; to realize that the gift and knowledge of Jesus is worth far more than an antique car or an old set of books or the family business.

May our families be those that prize Jesus above all things and be motivated by that to run hard, making sure we, the children, do the same. A. W Tozer says that lack of foundational faith is due to the decline of knowing who God is.

Let's change that.

Let's make our homes places that teach and model Jesus just as much as church buildings because life happens in the home.

This is where we understand what is important and what isn't, what has value and what doesn't.

And He alone has lasting generational value.

Infinite.

Abundant.

Eternal.

L|5

•••• •

CHAPTER FIVE
WORDS

She sounded like a hound dog.

Her voice booming through the woods.

I didn't have a clue where she was but I could hear her.

And so could he.

If you've ever had the chance to attend a cross-country meet, you know there's not that much to watch and not that much to do. The majority of the 3.1 miles takes place beyond visibility, through the thickness of nearby woods. Coaches, fans, and family may see the runners come into sight for a brief few seconds only to disappear quickly for the next eight minutes. The most exhilarating moment for the bystander is the firing of the starting gun, after which runners fade into the scenery of creation. The most visible portion of the race many times is the last two minutes.

A marvelous event to attend, am I right? The beginning and the end, that's what you have to work with. Knowing any details about the race beyond this is up to how far you yourself actually want to run. It's the only sporting event I know of where the spectator has to actually participate in some way to know what's happening during the majority of the event. Otherwise you get the first few seconds and the last few minutes.

The start.

And the finish.

I wasn't a competitive runner in high school and didn't do much of it for leisure either. I still have trouble enjoying the activity. The only reason I know any details about the sport is because my brother ran cross-country and track all four years of high school and during his years in college. We traveled all over the state watching him run in race after race after race. I just didn't understand it.

You just . . . run.

Through the woods.

Through mud.

Through water.

Through branches.

Throughout my brother's running career my mom did just as much running as he did. And every step of the way she carried in her hand her old, large, rusted, 36-inch high school cheerleading megaphone to cheer her son on throughout his three-mile trek through the woods. In the very beginning it was quite embarrassing for any of us standing near her. We kind of sidestepped away and went another direction.

She was loud.

But she stopped at nothing to unleash anthems of encouragement for my brother throughout his entire race, whether she knew he could hear her or not. She didn't know if he was in first place or last, whether he was bent over out of breath or in command of the race as if it was a mid-afternoon jog. It didn't matter. Constantly she ran, her voice pounding through the trees. It didn't matter where we were or who was there or how many runners were competing.

The picture of her running in and out of trees trying to spot my brother, never letting up her thunderous cheers, remains so vivid.

GO, STU!

LET'S GO BUDDY!

At one particular race I remember my aunt saying,

Pat, Stu can't hear you when he's deep in the woods. Why don't you let up a bit?"

Mom replied,

I don't know if he can hear me or not, but if he can, think how encouraged he'll be.

In my aunt's defense, as I said, this megaphone really amplified mom's voice for hundreds of acres. Your hearing just wasn't the same if at any point you were standing beside her when a shout came out.

Pat, do you have to yell so loud?

My uncle would say.

Mom quickly answered,

Yep!

She persisted with confidence.

GO STU!

After that race my aunt went up to my brother and asked,

Stu, when you were running on that trail, could you hear your mother cheering for you?

Oh, yes. I heard her the whole way.

I can hear her voice now.

The most interesting part of those races to me was much of what I have already described. We only got to see Stu start the race and then he was gone. Far too often the course was incredibly muddy and the weather unpleasant, so journeying through the woods was, for me, not something on my to-do list.

It was quite a different story for my mom. Nothing hindered her. Not rain, sleet, snow, mud, poison ivy, bears, nothing. A tornado couldn't stop her from chasing after my big brother. She entered those woods megaphone in-hand as if she was exploring the land of Narnia. Many times it felt like we saw less of her during the race than we did the actual runners.

She was on a mission.

She didn't have time to think about where Stu was in the pack before she lost sight of him. She didn't have time to think about whether he was tired or not. She didn't have time to think about if he'd come out on the other side leading the herd. She didn't have time to think about if her shoes would be ruined. She had 15 minutes to yell as loudly as she could, as hopefully as she could, as confidently as she could, as sweetly as she could before the race was over. It wasn't an issue of whether he could hear her or not. The reality for her was what her loud cheers would do for my brother *if* he could hear them.

My aunt later asked my brother what mom's cheering for him did for him as ran, hidden in the woods.

It makes me not want to quit. When my legs and lungs ache, when I feel like I'm going to throw up, I hear mom cheering, and it makes me want to keep going.

For my brother, the cheers of my mom while he ran changed potential outcomes of his race. There were times he wanted to stop. There were times he wanted to slow down. There were times he wanted to get sick. But he didn't. He continued. As he testifies, he pushed through much discomfort and physical pain because someone he loved and who loved him was in his corner fighting for him and encouraging him.

It's because words are a big deal.

Words communicate care and love and how we feel about certain things and how we feel about others.

Words can wreck us.

One sentence can let us know more than we want to know and one word can let us know truth that we are terrified to hear.

Because words are a big deal.

Especially those that come from our parents.

Author Haim G. Ginott writes,

*I possess tremendous power to make life miserable or joyous. I can be a tool of torture or an instrument of inspiration, I can humiliate or humor, hurt or heal.*14

Words can build up and they can tear down.

Words can bring promise or they can bring poison.

If you asked my brother about his running, mom's words did very different things for him than dad's words. Mom was proud and loving and uplifting. She'd raise his spirits and bring him to see the positives and not get upset with his race times or whether he finished first or third or fourth. Mom was a builder. She built with promise and care and concern. She was always a builder.

Dad was different.

Many days and nights dad seemed more like a one-man demolition crew. It felt like anything mom spent her time building up in us, dad came through and tore it down. He seemed like a giant wrecking ball. This transitioned mom out of building mode and into reconstruction and repair a lot of times. Mom was on cleanup duty during these days.

It was hard to feel secure or okay with anything we did or any accomplishment we made or our performance in school. We feared not measuring up and being short of what he wanted. He wanted perfection, but all I wanted was for him to be proud. I felt like a ship trying desperately to make headway, all the while unable to pull up the anchors. I wanted him to be honored and glad that I was his son. I didn't like feeling as if I was always a disappointment and that he was displeased with me.

I wanted him to be thankful for me.

For my brother, whether he won or lost, there was always something to be corrected or something to be said about his efforts from dad's eyes. Dad would constantly make suggestions about Stu's running. He'd say if Stu had only run a little bit faster on that last lap he could've won by 10 seconds instead of 5. Or maybe if he had run his last mile a couple seconds faster he might have beaten his personal record.

I always listened and felt so sad.

I wanted to scream.

I wanted to say

Are you serious? He just won the race by 35 seconds. Get off his back. You go run if you want to say so much!

My brother's accomplishments always fell short of my dad's standard. It didn't matter how many trophies or plaques or ribbons or medals Stu had hanging from his bookshelf. They weren't enough and a bookshelf full of them wouldn't be enough. There was no grace. There was no mercy. There was no love and there was no care. My brother told me one time that comments like that from dad usually just rolled off his shoulders. But he said there were always times when all he wanted was encouragement.

It's because we all do.

We all want a "Great Job!" not quickly followed by a "but."

I remember just wanting to know that I did a great job in his eyes. It didn't matter what it was. I just wanted to know that he was pleased with my efforts.

In his book *Hurt*, Chap Clark interviews countless teenagers that open up about their lives at home and the struggles they deal with on a daily basis. One of these students writes,

People think I have the "perfect" life. I wear the right clothes, I hang with the "cool crowd," my family has money. But the funny thing is, they don't know that I cry myself to sleep every night because my dad's expectations are impossible. I struggle with keeping up with school work. I come from a divorced home. They never see the real me. I have to put on a mask. I deal with the struggles of beer and alcohol. They don't know.15

Parents' expectations can hold us down and choke us slowly over time.

This weight is unbelievably hard to carry.

DISAPPOINTMENT

Homecoming.

The flowers and the parents and the names and the walking and the king and the queen.

You know the ordeal. All the seniors walk across the football field and meet their parents in the center and give their mom a flower and a kiss and shake their dad's hand. Then pose for an awkward picture that shows your parents dressed up really nice while you're all sweaty and gross in your football or soccer uniform. Then that picture stays around in the house for years.

What an experience.

And what a picture.

I have one of those pictures. And ironically, what I thought would be a picture of me and my mom in the center of the football field, just like the one of her and my sister just four years before on her senior year night, turned out to be a bit different. We had an extra person.

I looked up and 20 yards in front me there was mom . . . and dad.

What was he doing here? I was shocked and I didn't know what to think. I was floored. In the center of the football field in front of thousands of people, he surprised me.

This game could be our last home game of the season and could be my last time playing football at this stadium. Dad hadn't been to any of my football games that year, or the year before. It was an emotional moment for me. I didn't care how sweaty I was or how nicely he was dressed. I gave him one of the biggest hugs. I didn't care if I messed up his leather jacket or not. He was there. He was actually there.

And for just a split second, for a couple flashes of a camera, I felt whole.

In front of thousands of people and my entire football team, for that one moment that night, on one side was my mom and on the other side was my dad.

It was a complete picture.

It was a picture like almost everyone else's that night.

A child and two parents.

The flash of that camera did more than take a picture. It took a snapshot of my heart and my soul. This random picture on Homecoming night in 2003 was a representation of how I wished every other special occasion could have been: Me, sandwiched in between mom and dad, as the camera flashed.

But then the moment was over, the picture was taken, and we walked off the field. They went back up in the stands. The second half started and it was back to focusing on the game.

But I couldn't.

I still couldn't believe he was there.

Those two quarters felt like the fastest quarters that we played the whole season. Dad came down on the field after the game and gave me a hug. He said,

Son, great game! Too bad you didn't hit that last field goal or you would have had a perfect game!

There aren't any pads or helmets to keep words like that from hurting when it comes at you. And those words from dad off the field hit harder than anything on the field that night. It shrunk me down and I felt so small. It made me feel like showing up was a regret to him.

All I wanted to do was to please him and to believe that he thought I did a great job.

But his words were sharp.

They cut.

His words were blunt.

They pounded.

I walked into the locker room that night feeling like a failure, feeling like I let him down. My team won, but I lost. And just like that, my moment at center field was a distant memory of another time. Reality returned and I got in my car with my head down, covered in sweat and disappointment. I wanted to hear him say "great game" and leave it at that. I wanted to feel encouraged by my dad not torn down. I wanted him to let me know that he wanted to be there and that he was glad to be there and that he didn't want to be anywhere else that night.

But instead, I believed he found it unfortunate to travel all that way to watch his son come up short.

That night the exhaustion I felt from four quarters of football didn't come close to the exhaustion I felt from years and years of trying to meet my dad's expectations.

For my mom, if her parenting was a reflection of the treatment she received from her parents as she grew up, I can only believe that she knew what unconditional love and positive encouragement felt like. Her words were always uplifting. They were encouraging. They were affirming. They were full of life and they were full of promise.

All day.

Every day.

If I got an A on a test or paper, she was consistently more excited than I was. If I ever told her good news or any kind of news that she felt was exciting or great while on the phone with her, I would have to take the phone off of my ear because she screamed and yelled with joy so loudly.

My mom is crazy.

In a good way.

She never fails to mention how proud she is of me and how blessed she is to call me her son. It's words like that.

Phrases like that.

Things that let children know how blessed their parents are to have them as children and how proud they are. Words and phrases like that give children feelings that they cannot describe. I love knowing my mom delights in me.

That encourages.

Being compared doesn't.

Growing up, dad compared me to my brother constantly. He didn't understand that Stu and I were different. We had different personalities and different talents and different interests. Stu was brilliant in ways that I wasn't, and he enjoyed things that I didn't, and vice versa. That didn't seem to matter to dad. It appeared as if he wanted me to become Stu. It seemed he didn't like or appreciate the things I liked or was good at. It just always felt as if he wanted me to be that same brilliant student and that same star runner.

But that wasn't me.

I wondered if dad would be okay if I wasn't exceptional at anything. What if I was mediocre? What if I was average? If only parents understood that different children are different and they will perform differently outside the walls of the home. One child may be a star athlete and another may like music. And that's okay. The truth is, one child may not be exceptionally great at anything and one may be exceptionally great at many things.

Paul writes in Ephesians that we should encourage one another according to one another's need. It's vitally important to understand that the needs of different children are just as distinctive as the kids themselves. And encouragement from parents should be tailored to each situation.

For dad, he encouraged me to be like Stu. That didn't help. From him, I needed encouragement that was designed to encourage me for who I was and for the things I was interested in. Because children are unique. We are different. I am very different from both my brother and my sister. We are different in how we dress, how we act socially, the activities we're interested in, our music taste, our taste in food, our ambitions, our life goals, everything.

We are held together by the bond of love our mother tied around all of us, so that we love each other and have respect for the person each one of us is. We are tied together because we are family and we understand that we are not all identical. And the reality is, we don't wish we were all the same.

But growing up Stu was so smart, he was a gifted runner, he was the first-born. Stu was just the talk of the family. It was hard following in those shoes for me. But we knew who we were. We were different in our own way. But it cut so deeply when dad would say,

Why can't you be smart like your brother?

Why can't you act like your brother?

Why can't you eat over your plate like your brother?

Why can't you obey like your brother?

Because I am me, that's why. Dad, why can't you love me for being me, just me?

I thought my dad wanted to change me into someone else; someone who was easier for him to love. I believed he didn't love me as much as he did my brother. I believed I wasn't good enough. I believed I wasn't worth anything to him. This all came from the way he talked to me and the things he'd say to me.

Because words are a big deal.

John Eldredge tells this story in his one of his books:

There's a young boy named Charles who loved to play the piano, but his father and brothers were jocks. One day they came back from the gym to find him at the keyboard, and who knows what else had built up years of scorn and contempt in his father's soul, but his son received both barrels: 'You are such a faggot.'16

Words are powerful.

Words carry an enormous amount of emotional weight. They cause a lot of damage to a child's mind and self-worth. It's because children believe the words their parents say about them. It's incredibly hard for children to believe something different about themselves from what their parents believe. It seems impossible to break away and escape those words.

Those wounds.

If we hear we don't measure up, we believe it.

If we hear we aren't worth our parents' time, we believe it.

If we hear we should be a different person, we believe it.

But if we hear that we played well or that we're smart or that we look pretty or that it's okay to play the piano instead of hunt,

We believe it.

And the things my dad said to me that cut deeply and wounded me weren't always about sports. It was about knowing he cared and knowing he was there for us and that he enjoyed taking care of us. It was knowing that he wanted to be there and that he wanted to be in our lives. Many times it wasn't the negative things he'd say, it was the positive things and the reassuring things that he didn't say.

His reactions and the things he said let us know so much by his saying so little. How he processed things and how he responded showed us everything. Growing up I used to think that I wanted my dad to let me do whatever I wanted. I wanted mom to not care what time I came home or what I was doing or whom I was with. I thought that's what cool parents did. I thought that's what parents who really love their kids do: let them roam, free from discipline.

But that all changed in an instant.

It changed when I got a taste of what it felt like to have a parent not care about your reckless actions. In that moment I craved discipline and I craved a firm conversation. I craved for him to be disappointed in me.

Because I got caught that night.

I was 15.

I sat in the passenger seat as we drove down Sunset Avenue in silence. I stared at everything out the car window as if I would see something new. I stared at the restaurants and the grocery stores and the banks as if I hadn't been down this road once a day for as long as I could remember. I knew every building we would pass and when we would pass it. I knew when the Taco Bell was built and when the CVS showed up.

But there was nothing to do except look out the window.

No music.

No talking.

Silence.

I got found out that night. All my weekend lies and late night deception caught up with me and it all got exposed. My mom, defending me to friends at choir practice, looked so naïve because she had bought in to everything I told her. But all the stories and the fake sleepovers and the imaginary parties came crashing down that night in the choir room. Parents who caught wind of the real "weekend" me from their own children debunked all that mom thought she knew.

My expansive fictional narrative came to a close.

When we got home that night she made me tell her everything. I told her who and what and when and where. She could not believe I betrayed her trust the way I did. And as I look back, I can't either. Needless to say, I was grounded for quite some time. My behavior was going to be under tight surveillance from that point forward until I regained her trust.

All of that seemed warranted. It was fair. But then came the last requirement.

She said I had to call him.

I was terrified.

My fingers trembled as I dialed his number. I was certain my heartbeats were visible through my jacket. In my mind I just wished my mom didn't care. Why did I have to call him? Why was I grounded? Why couldn't I have parents who didn't mind me drinking? Why did my mom have to make such a big deal out of this? I wanted her not to be bothered about my actions. I wanted her to let it go.

Or so I thought.

Hello, dad? Um, I just needed to call you because I need to tell you that I got caught drinking. Mom wanted me to call and tell you myself and for you to know that it's been going on for a while and I have been lying to her about it. I'm sorry.

As I look back on memories I have of my father, many of them are tied to unforgettable moments when he said something so unexpected, when his words left me in utter disbelief.

This was one of those times.

Well, son, I can't say I am not disappointed.

If the sentence had stopped there it would have been an expected response, a normal response, a response that to me would have made perfect sense. But that wasn't all he said. He continued,

Son I can't say I am not disappointed because I wish you would have done it with me first.

Excuse me?

You're not disappointed because I got caught breaking the law drinking under age? You're not disappointed in me because of my reckless and thoughtless behavior? You're not disappointed in me because of my deceitfulness toward mom?

Rather, you're disappointed in me because I didn't think to share my first time getting drunk as a 15 year-old with my own father?

The conversation ended and I was speechless. I ran to my room and cried on my bed in my sleeping bag. This didn't feel like I thought it would. I was so perplexed and hurt. I felt worthless. It felt like my life didn't matter to him at all. Deep down I knew my behavior was reckless and wrong and at times life-threatening. But this didn't seem to do anything to him. It didn't bother him. He didn't care. How could this not affect him? It revealed to me that he believed I was capable of making my own decisions now apart from him.

But I didn't want to be apart from him.

I quickly realized that more than anything I wanted him to care. I actually wanted him to be upset with me. I wanted him to be disappointed in my actions, but for very different reasons than he gave. I wanted to be disciplined. I wanted him to ground me and to take away certain privileges. His words stuck with me. I played them over and over in my head. How did he really want that? In that moment, I wanted him to act like my dad, not my weekend drinking buddy.

His words have always held such a high value to me. But the thing is, I don't remember many of them, at least the positive ones anyway. What I remember most are his actions. I remember moments together. I remember Christmas. I remember holidays. I remember him cutting the grass in his red Chicago Bulls t-shirt. But amidst all the memories and the things I remember him doing and the words I remember him saying, the times I don't have memories about are the specific times he said he loved me or that he was proud or that he was just happy to be my dad.

I can't remember things like this, and maybe that's why when I look back it's so hard because the words I remember aren't words I really want to replay. The things that come to mind are the very things I wish I could erase and never think about again. Because you don't want to remember negativity when someone's gone. You don't want to only remember the bad things they said and realize the mental file labeled "Dad's encouragement" is totally empty. When they're gone, you want to think back on happy times and fun things.

But what do you do when you can't remember the good things? What do you do when the bad things consume every memory?

I remember him laughing. He laughed a lot. I loved hearing him laugh. I loved hearing him scream and yell at the TV during North Carolina basketball games. For every game he'd turn off the TV volume and cut on the radio, letting the voice of Carolina Basketball, Woody Durham, pound throughout the house and down the streets of the neighborhood since our windows were open. I can hear him yelling

Let's go boys!

You gotta make that!

Defense! Defense!

But these aren't the words and phrases that I want to remember necessarily. I wish I could remember him saying a lot more than directional commentary for Tar Heel sports. I wish I had something more in my mind, something more substantial and something with more feeling to remember. I wish there was something better to rewind and listen to over and over again.

Sadly, the thing that keeps on playing in my head, as I am sure it always will, isn't a time where he said he loved me or that he missed me or he wished he could see me. The thing repeated in my head for 11 years is the last set of words I heard him say.

And I wish I could forget them.

THE CALL

September of 2004.

There we were.

Sitting in the bar, silent, picking at the remains of an appetizer. He sat across from me, eyes focused on a nearby television. There was three feet of table in between us and I remember thinking how much I wished that slab of glossed wood was the only thing separating the two of us. I remember thinking how different things would be if that was all I was up against. I remember thinking how different life would be.

But it wasn't just a table. It was years. It was a closet full of memories that spanned miles. It was a lifetime of secrets. It was 19 years of unanswered questions. As I sat across the table from him, so many things ran through my mind. I wanted so many stones overturned. Where did he go? Why did he go? Did he think about me at all? Was it hard for him? Was I that unlovable? Were we that unlovable? And the question that never left, the one that occupied my mind more than any other; was it worth it? Not were we worth it. No. But was the whatever or whoever waiting for him when he closed the front door for the last time worth more than what he left behind, a family standing inside watching through the window as he drove away?

That was my question.

But there we sat. I remember him with his bleached blonde hair and a short sleeve button up shirt that resembled something from a hotel gift shop on some tropical island. But what did I know? Maybe it ended up in his suitcase after his private marriage ceremony in the Bahamas. Maybe it was something he picked up during one of those many trips he'd taken to the coast. Or perhaps it was a recent gift, a mere thank you, from the lady sitting next to him for the diamond tightly hugging her left ring finger.

A whole new set of questions emerged for me and in the midst of trying my hardest to push all the mental chaos aside, a tear began to roll down my cheek. I quickly wiped it, and any remnants of its existence, off my face. My efforts fell short as more began to come. With glossy eyes and moist cheeks I sat alone. They glared from across the table, their faces dressed in confusion. The more tears that fell the larger sense of mystery it seemed to create for them. The truth was I had seen that ring before, but not just once. You see, this ring was far more than a precious cut stone. This ring, this small trinket of finite value, had a very loud voice. With amplified sound this ring revealed that he was buying into something else. Someone else. He was chasing something different.

Something fresh.

Something new.

Throughout my life it always took different shapes. To me it seemed to be his way of starting over. It was his way of forgetting. But it was never small things. These were big things. They were flashy. They were exciting. They were exotic. Sometimes it would be a new house. Then maybe a new car. Maybe a new job would follow. A new boat. A new vacation home. A new dog. A new girlfriend. A new wife. A new family.

A new life.

He would erase and then he would replace. I remember thinking I had a price. I felt worthy of a constant substitute. I had a tough time comparing myself to a boat or a pure-bread chocolate lab. The weight found its way to my shoulders and slowly began to infiltrate the inner workings of my mind. In the end, the nightmare was not comparing myself to these things. It wasn't even believing my worth was less than theirs. It was much deeper than that. It was the simple truth that, by his actions, he showed that he believed I was inferior. It was a sobering reality to understand that he believed I could be replaced.

Me.

His flesh.

His blood.

His genes.

His family.

His son.

But inside, there was more to it than that. It wasn't just that he believed these things and demonstrated this in the way he continued to live his life. It went deeper. It hit harder. The truth came to me that he wanted to replace me. He was choosing to replace me. As time passed, it became harder and harder to understand. It's not exactly a thought you want to wrestle with. I remember thinking times were so different. As a very young child things weren't always this way. There were no complexities. There was no layered confusion. He was the center of my universe and for a time it seemed as if I was the center of his.

As I sat there in the booth crying, I will never forget the words that broke the silence.

What's wrong?

I froze. I thought about saying so many different things, but my thoughts were moving too fast and the sheer volume of them was too great. I tried to answer, but nothing came out. I stuttered. I tried to regroup and process his question again. During all those years, I was never honest concerning anything that I, or we as a family, went through after he left. To be honest, I had never planned on it. I believed bringing such things into the light would bring little change, if any at all, to our situation. But for some reason in that moment at Outback Steakhouse, I felt this inexplicable sense of urgency to be real with him.

An urgency to be honest. It was as if someone was easing me along, whispering,

It's time. It's time.

Whether it was time or not, I took a leap, and to this day, there's no question that choosing to be open with my father in that moment, changed his life and mine.

Maybe just mine.

Like an old, worn-down rope, I unraveled. I told him everything. Everything he wanted to know and everything he didn't. I spoke openly about how we, his children, needed him and had needed him for so many years. We wanted him around. We wanted him in our lives. We wanted him to love us. We needed him to love us. I shared vulnerably of how we missed him. How I missed him.

Following my very wet, sniffling, and jumbled monologue, a woman's voice towered above all the restaurant ambiance:

Jonathan, you're 19 years-old, a freshman in college. You don't need your father. You're an adult.

I remember being so startled and confused. I couldn't breathe. I looked over into my dad's eyes as he sat there with a facial expression that let me know he was in full agreement. What did they mean I didn't need him? What do I say now? What could I say? I had absolutely nothing. Words seemed foreign and inadequate. As they continued talking all I could hear amidst the clutter of their words was . . .

Son, I'm leaving you. Again. No need to worry though, you should be fine.

With tears filling my eyes I quickly got up from the table and ran to the car. With my head in my hands I stood sobbing. What was he trying to say? More importantly, what did he want me to say? That I was okay with him continuing to be a shadow in my life?

It broke me.

This, very different from the previous car ride I mentioned, was silent as well. On the same road. Passing the same buildings. But this time I wasn't looking out the window. My eyes were closed in the back seat, coated with salty tears. He dropped me off and I ran inside straight to my bedroom. I could hear him tell my mom that I might still need to be in counseling.

I couldn't believe it.

In that whole time at dinner what he got was that there were some serious problems with me that needed to be dealt with. Apparently he didn't think anything of his own words and the things he said to me.

A few days later I got a phone call from him. I was sitting in my dorm room working on some last minute homework when the phone rang. When I answered, he didn't sound very happy.

And he wasn't.

He told me how upset and disappointed he was in me that I shared with mom the details of our dinner at Outback just a few evenings before. I didn't understand why he was so angry. But I never got the chance to say anything before he hung up. And I will never forget those last words:

Son, if you ever have something you want to talk to me about and don't want your mother to know I suggest you not bring it up because you better count on me doing the exact same thing to you that you did to me.

Click.

Each day that followed I wondered if he'd call me. I waited with anxiety as if it was Christmas Eve and I was five years-old again. Days turned into weeks, and weeks rolled into months and months to years. I soon realized there was a difference between that phone call I longed for and Christmas Day: Christmas comes every year. It's always on time. It's always inevitable. It's certain. It will come.

Eleven years have gone by and I haven't heard his voice since that September. It's been 11 years since I've heard words from his mouth. Eleven years since I've seen words from him on a piece of paper. Sometimes I wonder if I'd recognize his voice now if I heard it. I wonder if I heard his laugh would I know it's his.

But all that is silly.

I'll never forget his laugh.

I'll never forget his voice.

I'll never forget his words.

Never.

L|6

●●●●　●

CHAPTER SIX
STRINGS

I hated that ruler.

I despised it.

And I had just as much bitterness and resentment toward the alien or robot or lion or superhero that held it. That statue with that ruler was a glaring display that I didn't have the credentials. I didn't have what it took. I was lacking. I didn't meet the mark. It told me to come back next year.

It told me I was short.

Literally.

That cartoon character just stood there, motionless and never blinking but always smiling, telling me I couldn't get on the roller coaster. That smile made me feel as if they were pleased to show me that I couldn't get on; pleased to show me that I was too short.

No matter how many inches or centimeters shy I was of the requirement, it felt so far out of reach. I felt like I'd never be that tall and I'd never get to ride the Vortex.

Five feet?

You have to be five feet tall?

Professional basketball players aren't even five feet tall!

That was me. I'm sure you've been there. You'd stand back, feet on the pavement, while your friends' and families' feet were high in the air, floating above you as they flew in and out of a volcano or something resembling Bruce Banner's science lab.

You saw everything.

But weren't a part of anything.

You wanted so badly to get on and have that ride of your life. You wanted the park just to let you on and be with your family. You didn't want some cartoon animal telling you to go off and grow a few inches and come back. What was wrong with how tall you were then, in that moment?

Afterwards, everybody got off and came down with their hair every which way, out of breath, talking as if they just were taken to Saturn and back. You walked beside them with your head down, eating your funnel cake or corn dog or turkey leg. Or maybe you were staring at the caricature of yourself that you got your parents to pay for as an appeasement to you for not getting to ride the roller coaster that Tom Cruise's time in the Navy inspired.

You were sad because roller coasters are fun. They're exhilarating. They're a thrill.

Because people love roller coasters.

They take us back to simpler times and for just a short few seconds or minutes we feel like it's the most fun we've ever had. People pay hundreds of dollars to spend the day riding them while getting the worst farmer's tan of their life. Not only that, you wait in line for hours upon hours upon hours just to ride a roller coaster that lasts 35 seconds. As a result, your days at theme parks are spent more in line than they are on actual rides.

But you love it.

At least once you're tall enough.

That's the part that isn't appealing, the fact that the fun in a theme park has contingencies. You have to be this tall or weigh this much. Sure, you can go ride the teacups all day but no one wants that. You want to ride the coasters and the main attraction rides. You want to ride that one ride everyone talks about and the one that will leave you talking about it for the next year. You want the one that you get off of only to spring back down the stairs to get in the very same line.

Because you want to ride in the middle this time.

Then in the front car.

But then in the last car.

Then you want to sit with your brother.

Then your sister next time.

You try all these different combinations and arrangements and each time feels different. You have worn that ride out. But the thing is, you're going to come back in the next several months and feel like you've never ridden that ride before in your life. It will be the first one you get in line for.

Until a new ride gets built.

Then you slowly but surely drift away from your once favorite ride to the new and improved, shiny and glimmering, faster and taller, one with more twists and more turns, coaster. What the ruler did to you for a season you now do to the old, wooden, rickety, bumpy grandpa roller coaster. You forget about it because it doesn't have what it takes. You forsake your once favorite ride because it doesn't measure up. It's not

Newer.

Faster.

More dangerous.

And just like that your fun transfers. Because we all have our own qualifications and standards on what makes a ride fun to us. What makes it exhilarating and worth the wait. And that's the key. Was it worth it? Was the waiting in line and the sweating and the leaning on the rails and the hours worth it? Was it worth the time or was it a waste of time?

We've all stood below the tracks that bend and twist and barrel roll above us, putting our wallets back in our pockets and our belts back on and tucking our shirts back in. We've talked amongst the group, listing off the pros and cons of the ride that just took us through Gotham City. We've talked about how the coaster did this but it didn't do that and how we loved this part but that part wasn't as fast and this bar hurt our legs but that bar made me feel safe. It goes on and on.

This happened to me at a theme park in North Carolina when I was little, except I wasn't involved in the critique. Rejected by the alien robot, I watched as dad, Stu, and Grace Anne rushed off and got in line for the Vortex while mom took me to the swings. But the swings weren't the Vortex. It was big and red and it looped and twirled all over the place. The swings didn't do that. They just went around and around and around and around. After the ride, the height-qualified members of my family came back down to earth and talked and talked and talked about it.

Guys, I'm right here.

They loved that ride. But time passed and other coasters got built and the Vortex became old news. What used to be their favorite attraction now was the subject of a "hey, remember when . . ." story. Dad took them on other rides and it made sense that it wasn't always the Vortex that they continued to talk about.

Theme parks grow and theme parks change and get bigger and better.

However, what I never saw coming was that something would come along outside of that theme park that was cooler and more fun and more special to my dad than we were. I never thought that we wouldn't be the people he spent family days with. I never thought he would get bored with us and move on. I never thought my dad would turn into the cartoon bear with the ruler, telling us we didn't have what it took to ride life with him.

And I never thought we'd become the old, bumpy roller coaster that was forgotten about, passed up for something better.

TIED

There's this street in Central London.

It's a pretty famous street, known for its fine quality of men's tailoring. Suits, shirts, pants, tuxedos. It's seen its share of famous customers over the years. Built in the 18th century, tailors set up shop and have been around on that street ever since.

Savile Row.

Now, I've never been there nor will I ever be able to buy anything on that street. I don't belong on Savile Row. I don't have the clothes or the notoriety or any of that. I don't know the lingo well enough in the fashion world to even pretend that I belong on that street. You might feel the same. It's another world. Another language.

But not entirely.

You see, tailors on Savile Row have a way of describing the cloth they receive from the cloth merchants and part of this language includes a phrase that is familiar to us all.

No strings attached.

Aside from *NSYNC's 2000 album release, this phrase means something to us. We use this in common conversation. We use it in Wal-Mart at the same time tailors are using it in London on Savile Row.

But back to London.

When sending material to the tailors, cloth merchants will tie a tiny piece of white string on the edge of the cloth, indicating a flaw in the weave. You get that? Cloth merchants will tie strings to pieces of cloth that locate the flaws in their weaves.

Even tiny flaws.

And so it goes on Savile Row, whenever a tailor needs a perfect, flawless, immaculate, pure piece of cloth, they simply say to the merchant,

Four meters of silk, no strings attached.

That's a beautiful picture. But it's also a tough picture.

It's tough because that piece of cloth is me. Just like those faulty pieces of cloth with all their strings, I've got imperfections. I have strings tied everywhere. And it's hard because sometimes you don't feel lovable or worth anyone's time. You look in the mirror and all you can see is string after string after string, tied so tightly around your most insecure shortcomings.

My dad's words and how he spoke to me made me feel like that's all he saw. His words conveyed a much larger truth. His words showed me that it wasn't just that I didn't measure up; they showed me what he was looking for and that he was moving on. I felt that, when he looked at me and when he was making his decision to leave or to stay, he focused on the strings tied around my hands and feet and neck and the strings tied to my brother and my sister and my mom. Seeing them in mass quantities, he took off. We were faulty. We had a squeaky wheel. We were the old roller coaster that wasn't fun anymore. Familiarity had bred contempt.

Away he went, taking his ruler with him, the ruler that let me know I had too many strings attached to me. I wasn't a perfect piece of silk or cotton or wool. I was delivered with an abundance of strings to his front door.

And he needed something different.

I was the Vortex, enough fun for a while but not forever.

Jesus tells a story in the Luke's gospel about a father who never moved on from loving his son, even in spite of all the son's flaws.17

This younger son goes to his father and demands his inheritance early. He grabs all that is owed to him and books it out of town, leaving his father and his older brother and their home in his rear view. The son wastes away all his money and, after all is gone and a famine strikes, he finds himself in great need. After all he had done and after disgracing his family, he is stuck.

He is on his own.

And he has nothing left.

In his despair, the son decides to return home in hopes of being hired on as a servant in his father's house. For he knows, even his father's servants are living better and having more food than he is at that moment. As Jesus continues, He says that the son was on the dirt path that led to his house. He made the turn onto his road and was still a good distance away from the front porch.

But his father saw him.

His dad got up off the porch and ran down the road and grabbed him and hugged him. Jesus says that the father embraced his son and kissed him. After this, the son broke down and confessed to his father his mistakes and how he was wrong. He says

Father, I have sinned against heaven and against you! I am unworthy to even be called your son!

This son felt bad. He knew what he had done was wrong.

This son was greatly aware of his strings.

But Jesus continues. He says the father ignores it all and orders his servants to grab the most important animal on the land and kill it for dinner. He orders them to get his boy some clean clothes and a ring for his finger and some shoes. They have a feast. They celebrate the return of the son who ran away and abandoned his family.

This son basically spit in his father's face. Yet he comes back and his father calls everything to a halt in order to celebrate his youngest son's return. The father doesn't care what happened. He hasn't been on the porch stewing over all his son had done or thought about the ways he was going to punish him for it all. The father does none of that.

The father loves him, embraces him, and provides for him in ways that don't keep record of strings. He loves him unconditionally. His father cares for him in spite of his flaws and his shortcomings. Can you imagine the son's apology? I imagine he said something like this,

Father, I realize that I never acknowledged all that you had done for me. You were always there and you always provided more than enough for me. I understand that I never reached that point but I am here now to say I am sorry and that my eyes are now open to the reality of all that you do as my father. I am on my knees begging your forgiveness and I am fine with being hired on as your servant because I just want to be with you and I want to tell you what happened to me and where I've been because I have no one else.

The son knew his flaws. He knew he messed up. And when he was out in the real world and no one gave him anything and no one was there for him, there was something inside him that knew he could return home.

No one lent him a hand.

No one fed him.

No one gave him a place to stay.

No one listened.

But he went home and his father ignited a celebration for his lost, believed-to-be-dead son's return. That's grace. That's forgiveness. That's mercy. That's unconditional love.

That's love in the face of tightly tied strings.

That's the love and mercy of a parent, who before his son was born, knew that kids would be kids and that his son might never understand the extent of his father's love. He knew that this would happen. He knew that he would be taken for granted. He knew that he would be taken advantage of. But he stuck it out because this was his son.

And I'm sure that at the celebration the son looked his dad in the eye and said,

Dad, I have so much to tell you and I just need someone to listen. I have been to hell and back and I have so much on my heart that I need to let out. Can we talk?

I imagine the father then looked his son in the eye and said,

Son, I've been sitting on that porch rocking back and forth ever since you left, waiting for you to come home. I will always be here for you no matter what happens. My shoulder will always be here for you to lean on and my ears will always be open to anything you need to say. So yes, you can come to me with anything in the world and I will listen. Take all the time you need.

I am here.

For as long as I can remember, I have heard that account from Luke and wanted that to be me. I wanted to be coming home from school or getting out of the car and have my dad run out the door and grab me and hug me. I wanted him to do that on the weekends we'd go to see him. I wanted him to be so excited because he hadn't seen me for two weeks and he just wanted to squeeze me and not want to let go. I wanted the dad from Jesus' parable to be my dad.

I understood that the reason Jesus told that parable was to direct the listeners' attention to the Father and how we are truly accepted and loved and cared for; not on the basis of what we've done or how we've messed up or failed, but on the basis of Jesus and what He's done.

I knew that.

But even still, I wanted to be run after and grabbed and picked up and squeezed.

I wanted to know that, even though I had done so much wrong and failed at so many things, dad didn't care. He wanted to celebrate anyway. He wanted to love me anyway. I wanted to come home to that.

Several years ago when I was in college a friend of mine told me he had to move out of his dad's house and into his mom's house for a while. He also said that before moving in with his mom he lived at a friend's house for several months. When I asked him why all the moving he told me his dad kicked him out of the house because he wasn't getting along well with his dad's new girlfriend.

I was kicked out of my dad's house . . . by my dad. I couldn't believe it.

My friend told me it felt like he wasn't important to his dad anymore. He said it felt like his dad moved on.

So what about the prodigals who can't go home?

What about the ones who were kicked out?

What about the ones who were left behind when their mom took their sister and brother and left the state?

What then?

Where do they go?

What do they do with their strings?

What about those whose strings are just too big to look past and the ones whose parents choke them with their faulty strings?

I wanted my dad to stop looking at my faults and my inconsistencies and just love me in the midst of them. I wanted him to say they didn't matter. I wanted him to break the ruler. I wanted his love to be given freely because I was his son, not because I performed well or did what he wanted me to do all the time or because I was perfect. Because I wasn't.

I wanted to be important to him even if I messed up. I wanted to be valuable to him on the basis of who I was not on what I did.

I wanted to be the shiny new roller coaster.

I wanted to be worth all the hardship, whatever he believed that to be.

Dad, pick me.

Choose me.

Love me.

Pick me over the better and more exciting life you are chasing. Choose me over the women you search for and drive to see. Pick me over the cars and the houses and the boats and the jobs and the money. Love me more than you love those things. Love me that way. Love me because I am your son and your family. You used to make me think I was more important than all those things. Love me because you want to. Love me because I am me and nothing else.

Every single ounce of me wants to be loved by my dad. And not just loved, but loved with every single piece of baggage I carry and every single piece of string I have tied to me. I know I have blown it so many times and the baggage I have won't even fit on the plane. I know I am stuck with them. The strings are tied. They're a part of me.

Over the years, while sitting down with college students and talking about the messiness of their families and sifting through the wreckage, so many of them have told me how much they wish their parents would love them unconditionally, free from expectations and contingencies.

We know we're tough to deal with.

Children know this.

A senior in high school once said to me,

I want my parents to love me even when times are tough, no matter what.

We know we have strings tied everywhere possible and some in places no one can see. That's the reality we live in and we are so terrified someone will find them. And once they do, they will pack their bags and flee the scene.

Because that's what has happened in our families.

We all have those thoughts. Thoughts that maybe if we were different and maybe if we didn't mess up that our parents would stick around. We think that maybe our homes would work out differently if they were free from faults, failures, and infrequencies.

Maybe if I run faster he'll love me.

Maybe if I lose these last few pounds mom will want to hug me again.

Maybe if I have a 4.0 GPA they'll be proud of me again.

Maybe if I'm accepted to this school they'll forget about the party last week.

Maybe.

Living under the weight of "maybe . . ." is exhausting.

Navigating life through the wreckage of so many past and present train wrecks takes a toll on us. And when we can't find this love and this acceptance at home we go looking for it elsewhere. We begin looking in those last places that deep down in our hearts we don't want to look. We know it's not what we're looking for but we look anyway. We look because others claimed those things to be the answer. We look because other friends told us it was worth it and would make us feel good. And when that happens the majority of the time the results aren't great.

We look because every single one of us needs it. We desperately need it.

As a kid, I wanted that kind of love and affection because I knew myself too well. I knew who I was and what I believed I had to offer. In the midst of it all, in the midst of everything going on at home with my dad, he made me believe that no one would think twice about loving me for who I was. When he left, I didn't think anyone would look past the things I had done or the things I hadn't done because I knew that he didn't. I felt ashamed. I didn't think things would get better. I just wanted a dad that would love on me and say that nothing would ever get in the way of his love for me. That no matter what, I could count on him being there.

Because I, like most children of divorce, thought that it was something I did that was the reason for his leaving. I thought he left because of me. I made claims that I would be a better child and that I would do better in school. I promised to do more chores and help around the house and go to bed when I should and keep my room clean.

I was desperate.

Children are desperate.

We'll do anything to keep mom or dad at home. We'll do anything to keep our family together. We'll do anything to know that our parents are going to stay. We'll do anything to keep things the way they are. We do this because we know, once one of our parents walk out the door, our world will be rocked. We know our world is about to change, forever. Because of this, we question whether or not love will exist in this new way of life with only one parent around. We question these things because we believe that love from our parents is contingent on our performance. This is true for so many stories.

We believe we are the problem.

And it's because parents say that. Like the friend of mine who once told me,

My mom yelled at me last night and told me that I am the reason she and my dad fight, that I am the reason our family is falling apart.

I wanted to believe that it wasn't me that made dad leave, but no matter what he said and how he said it, I always believed it was me. Even now.

It's because he traded us. He traded us for something else.

He traded us for something more entertaining.

Something less faulty.

Something less squeaky.

I felt like a rented movie, taken back to avoid any late fees. I felt like a movie that had been watched too many times. I can't say how vital my mom was during these seasons and during these times of emotional need that I went through, even if in the moment I didn't realize it.

I don't think a day has gone by since I was born that I have not heard the words "I love you" come out of my mom's mouth directed to me or written in an email or a text or a note. Because of that, I don't think a day has gone by since I was born that I questioned whether or not my mom loved me with every part of her being. It's an undeniable fact for me. And others who know her would say the very same thing.

She loves her children more than anything.

Some days I think about how I would have turned out if I hadn't had a mom who walked behind my dad, cleaning up the mess the best way she knew how. She voices her love for me daily, by the hour sometimes. I could be in a meeting or busy driving and get a voicemail from her saying how much she loves me. Sometimes I laugh to myself because I just can't understand it.

I don't think I ever will.

Not only does mom convey to me and to my brother and sister her love by her words, she reveals it in action and all that she does. It's because words can't exist alone. They need movement. They need to be tangible. And as a kid, I was dependent on both. When I lived at home, mom would demand from me around 15 hugs a day. She was and still is all about some hugs.

And lately, I've been thinking about her hugs. Yes, of course she wants hugs from me. But I think also that she *needs* hugs from me. And I've never thought about that before. Growing up, I never thought that the parent needed hugs. I always thought it was me. I never thought about her needing a hug from me.

But she does.

She needs to hug her child. She needs that part of our relationship. It's incomplete without it. She needs for me to know that she loves me and that she loves letting me know that by hugging me. She would always come to my bedside at night and say,

You didn't hug me before you went to bed.

I would always try to just reach out my hands in a very sloppy manner but no, she would tell me to sit up and give her a "good" hug.

I would not trade my mom's hugs for anything.

They conveyed so much and still do. They disarmed my defenses and allowed me to breathe. Her hugs and how she loved us let me know she looked past the strings I had dangling off of me.

Children need this kind of love, support, and care.

We want hugs. We want goodnight kisses. We want back rubs. We want to be tucked in. We want to be loved on. We want to be needed. We want you to need us and to be around us because we are your children and you love us. We want to know we are worth your time and your energy. We want to know you value us. And when the going gets tough we are praying desperately that you don't get going. We want you to love us before we have everything figured out. We need you to love us during the process, during our mistakes and our pitfalls.

In the book of Luke, Jesus was passing through the town of Jericho. There was a tax collector there by the name of Zacchaeus. Not only was he a tax collector, he was the chief tax collector and was doing quite well for himself. Now, we know already that, due to his title, his source of income, he is not looked upon too highly by his fellow neighbors and others in the city. He takes their money. Would you like him?

Luke tells us that as Jesus entered the town, Zacchaeus wanted to see who Jesus was. I am sure Zacchaeus heard things about this man they called Jesus. He heard of His miracles and he heard of His teachings. Zacchaeus wasn't just looking to see what Jesus looked like from the top of this tree. He wanted to see Him for who He was. Later in Luke's account he says that Jesus walked up to the tree and told Zacchaeus to get down because He wanted to have lunch with him at his house.

After this, after their lunch and after being with Jesus, Zacchaeus told Him that he was giving back half of his possessions to the poor and for those he had defrauded, he would return fourfold for what he took.

He was a changed man.

Why?

Why did Zacchaeus have a complete turnaround just because Jesus wanted to come visit him and have a sandwich?

Because he not only saw Jesus, he *experienced* Jesus.

In that moment he not only saw Jesus for who He really was, Zacchaeus experienced who Jesus really was. He experienced the unconditional love that Jesus offered. It wasn't hearsay anymore. It wasn't talk around town. It was words fulfilled. Jesus didn't come to Zacchaeus and tell him to give back half of his things to the poor and to restore those who he defrauded four times and then Jesus would come over for a bite to eat.

No.

Jesus came before all that. Jesus entered into Zacchaeus' mess before the mess was gone. Jesus came to Zacchaeus and looked past his failures. He met him where he was. He came to a broken, flawed, thief.

He looked past his strings.

Jesus comes to us that way. He comes to us in the midst of our despair and in the midst of our sin. Jesus wades right in the middle.

But in our world we fail so miserably to know this kind of love, to feel this love, to experience this love. The truth is, the way we want it and the way we need it won't come from our dad that left and it won't come from the mom that didn't come back from the grocery store. It comes from the Person that came and gave His life to put on full display that love like that is real.

But it's hard.

It's hard because it seems that love like that isn't available. Many start to look at this man Jesus the same way they look at the parent who left. It's the same way they look at the one who stayed but is never there. The same way they look at the two parents who left them in the chair on the front porch of somebody else's house.

Another high school student interviewed by Chap Clark writes,

I was two when my dad walked out on me and my mom. Sure, I saw him a lot, but it hurt. I never saw him again after fourth grade. He stopped calling and writing. My mom remarried the summer after fifth grade. I hated him. In sixth grade I lost my virginity. I just wanted to be loved by a guy. I hated my life, but when I had sex I felt like I was cared about and loved. I slept with three guys. Then in seventh I started to do drugs and drink. I would go to parties and stay out late. My mom kicked my stepdad out, so I was happy. School started. I was smoking and drinking a little here and there. I didn't really feel loved or cared about. I felt dead inside. I picked up cutting. When I saw myself bleed, I just felt so alive. To feel the pain was the best feeling I could feel. My mom found out, so I stopped because I had to see a counselor. A few months later I stopped eating. I had to be perfect. I was the worst daughter. I had bad grades. I had a bad attitude. My dad wasn't around. I felt like I was worthless. I wasn't good enough for him. I feel like my life is worthless. I just want to die half the time. I want to feel like I'm worth something, loved, and cared for. Where do I find that?18

We struggle to believe we are loved and cared for because we look to the way our parents have treated us, how they left us, and how they traded us for brighter and shinier things.

But even in our struggle, we must learn to hope in the Scriptures that tell us the very reason we know this love exists is because of Jesus. It is because Jesus came and died. It's only by His death and defeat of death that our strings get untied. He's the only one with scissors for our strings.

Whether we think we find unconditional love in this life or not, from our parents, our boyfriends, our girlfriends, our husbands, our wives, our social groups, our sports teams, our academic clubs, our teachers, whomever it is, we must know that One person,

a Man,

a Savior,

a Friend,

gave up His life so we would know that only His love is unconditional. And not only does it exist but it's fully available. It's available for the motherless, the fatherless, the broken, the torn, the tired, the lost causes, and every single version of the flawed, wretched, human condition.

And that's all of us.

That's you.

That's me.

L|7

●●●● ●

CHAPTER SEVEN
FILLED

726.

727.

728.

729.

730.

Over 730 days.

Two years.

It had been two years since that September afternoon phone call.

I'd count the days as they passed, each day another day of silence. It was hard. I always envisioned my dad being a part of my life as I made my way through college. I always pictured him coming to visit me and us going to football games and him helping me with schoolwork. I thought about him moving me in to my first off-campus house or apartment and helping with any repairs to fix up the place.

But the clock was ticking.

I was halfway through my junior year and he hadn't been to visit.

Sitting in the kitchen with my sister that Thanksgiving in 2006, we talked about dad. I shared how I missed him and wished for things to be different. I told her how all I wanted was to know that he and I would talk again and that some time in the future we'd have a restored relationship. I longed for that. I wanted to know he'd be at my graduation and then he'd be at my wedding one day and then later down the road he'd be at the hospital for the birth of my first child.

I wanted all these things.

I wished for all these things.

But then, after grabbing some chips out of the pantry, my sister turned around and looked at me and asked me some of the hardest questions ever asked to me. As tears welled up in her eyes, she struggled to say,

Jonathan, what if things don't ever change?

What if everything stays the way it is right now and life doesn't go back to how it was?

What if you don't speak to dad again?

What will you do?

Will you be okay with that?

These were such heavy questions. They caught me off guard. But no matter how surprised I was, I knew my answer.

No.

No, I wouldn't be okay with that.

I remember thinking that I'd be so angry and so bitter. I wanted him back in my life. I wanted to see him again and to talk to him again so badly that I didn't care how much it was eating away at my heart and mind. I couldn't imagine what it would be like for him to never be a part of my life again.

Maybe that is you too.

You may be reading for many reasons. Maybe one of them is to find answers. Maybe your children are lost in a clouded daze caused by the split between you and your spouse. What you believed to be a matter strictly between parents has now spilled over and reached the lives of your kids. With your hands raised high, you cry out from the depths of your own soul for help. You cry out for answers.

Or maybe you are sitting where I once sat. Maybe you are trying to find answers to something that, to you, has always been a mystery. No matter how hard you try, you fail to make any sense of your childhood. You wonder if you ever will. Nightly you find yourself on your knees, at your bedside, praying for restoration, praying for healing.

Praying for anything.

Hopefully answers.

But my journey didn't do what I thought it would. I thought that understanding why my dad left my family would bring me peace and closure and all sorts of things. I thought uncovering the great mystery of my life concerning my parents' divorce would give me rest. But it didn't. I didn't get clarity and I never got any special kind of news report. The answers never came, at least ones that I was satisfied with.

I was angry.

I was desperate.

And I didn't want anything to do with Jesus.

ANGRY

In the months after my dad hung up that phone, I processed his actions differently as time continued on. There were months of ignoring. There were months of much grief and brokenness. There were months of anger and streams of bitterness. There were months of confusion. And, finally, there were many months of apathy. I didn't know how to think about it. I didn't know what was normal. I had to train myself in new patterns of thinking; patterns very different and foreign from those I learned when he left for the first time more than a decade prior to that September in 2004. Not knowing where to go from there, I fully embraced an apathetic attitude.

If it doesn't matter to him, why should it matter to me?

I was determined not to let this man affect my life in even the slightest way since he viewed my absence from his life about as significant as a mere paper cut.

Resentment grew.

Frustration and coldness planted themselves firmly in my heart. I wanted badly for him to know my anger. I wanted him to know I was accomplishing things just fine without him. I wanted him to know his removal from my world proved to be anything but an obstacle. I thought of the ways to let him know these things. I thought of writing him a letter. I thought of calling him. I thought of obtaining his address and driving to his house unannounced. I wondered what he would say. I wondered about the look on his face when he saw mine. How would he react knowing that his absence had not ruined my life completely? Would he be disappointed at all? A more pressing question was, would he even let me in the door?

Thinking back to these days and these thoughts, it's frightening to see and be able to feel the amount of pride I had in my heart towards my father. I wanted so terribly for him to be unsuccessful in hurting me. I harbored a great deal of anger and built up thick walls around the tender parts of my heart and soul; making sure to protect myself from the pain. Sadly, this was pain I knew to be inevitable. Fully cognizant, I still plowed ahead. So much of my heart wanted nothing to do with that portion of my life.

The reality was, and still is, my heart could not be separated from him. I was ignorant to believe that compartmentalizing was possible. I was naïve to think there was just one area where the effects of my relationship with him had leaked. There was such a tremendous amount of pride within me, I was blinded to the truth that this was affecting all aspects of my being.

It was controlling me.

From hundreds of miles away and several years removed he was controlling me. All of these years, this was the truth I was terrified to acknowledge. I dreaded the day I would look into the mirror and admit to myself that I was still hurting. I felt so weak weeping, knowing I wept tears of brokenness that fell from clouds formed by this particular storm in my life. This storm had been making its way through every area of my life for so long. It was this storm that, with its powerful winds and rains, had beaten me down. I had nothing left. I was tired. I became overwhelmed by a sense of being lost and of a lack of strength. There were times I wanted to give up. I wanted to raise a white flag and simply give him the victory. I wanted to tell him he won. I wanted to tell him he beat me. I thought that maybe if I surrendered, the pain would stop and I could breathe again. I longed for relief.

In this season of despair and depression I deeply wanted to know that someone understood. I wanted to know that I wasn't alone. I wanted to know that someone else felt this way. I wanted to know that there was someone else who grieved this way.

I wanted to believe that there was someone else.

Anyone.

It was very hard to cling to the open arms of Jesus. I struggled to believe He was comfort. I struggled to believe He was peace. I struggled to believe He was love. Above all, I struggled to believe He was sovereign. I understood and firmly believed He held the world in His hands, but it didn't seem that included mine. The cute children's song seemed to be that and that alone: cute. I wanted to know that He held my world in His hands.

I doubted Him.

I didn't think He cared about my pain and my hurt.

This all stemmed from the fact that I compared Jesus to what I knew and what I experienced. I compared Him to my circumstances.

In his book, *Knowledge of the Holy*, A.W. Tozer explains that our concept and understanding of God is somewhat hindered because He is immaterial and uncreated, yet all we know and can comprehend are things that are material and created.19 For this reason, when we describe Him we use material language and material concepts. We are forced to compare God to things we know and see and experience because our minds do not have categories for Him. We can't fathom something or someone to be truly eternal and truly created from nothing.

Tozer explains that it is impossible for humans, material and created things, to think of God and describe Him outside of these paradigms. This helps us see why our earthly families are set up the way they are. Our parents provide us with a material understanding of the concept of a Father and a Protector and a Comforter. Our families are designed to help us find meaning for these concepts and attributes that pertain to God, including love and sacrifice. Our families are designed to direct our attention toward and develop our affections for our Sovereign God. Our families are to be institutions that help grow our love for the King.

Sadly, the very agents He desires to use within the family to show who He is and His character are the very agents hindering His children from learning, knowing, and experiencing His love and care.

As a child crippled by divorce, my work was cut out for me. I had to work hard to prevent my earthly concept of father from affecting my view of my True Father. This wasn't easy. There were long years that I consistently lost the battle. It was hard not to let my dad and what he did to my family poison my view of the Savior. It was, and still is, an earnest battle of prayer that my mind and heart be protected from the deceit of sin. I have to understand that God invented the concept of rescue and His rescue mission began long before I stepped onto the scene and before my dad chose the path he did.

I have to believe that He had a plan and still does.

It's increasingly common for many children to have difficulty believing this because of so many unwelcomed obstacles placed in our paths; paths overgrown with abandonment. An evaluation of the roles and behaviors of the parents of this generation is very much needed. What if our parents' actions helped and gave value to the belief in a God of unending love, security, compassion, grace, and mercy? It is vital to understand that the role of earthly parents plays such a large part in a child's concept of who God is and what He came to do.

Family counselor, speaker, and author Paul Tripp writes,

There's an organic relationship between the seeds you plant and the fruit you harvest. In the physical world you will never plant peach pits and get apples. In the same way, there will be organic consistency between the seeds of words and actions that you plant in your relationships and the quality of harvest that you will experience later as you live and relate to one another. Every day you harvest relational plants that have come from the seeds of words and actions that you previously planted. And every day you plant seeds of words and actions that you will later harvest. Most of the seeds you plant will be small, but one thousand small seeds that grow up into trees will result in an environment-changing forest. Your relationships are continuously planted with little-moment seeds of words and actions, which grow into the forest of either love or trouble.20

The question with which to wrestle is, are we as children who have been left by our parents harvesting fruit that is saturated with the truth of the gospel or are we harvesting fruit absent of the truth of Jesus? What we know of God as Father, what we know of provision, protection, and care is directly related to what we see and experience in our families.

What I saw in my home deeply rattled me. It messed with what I believed and what I thought was normal. The way I saw my dad treat my mom, the way he walked out on us and on her, affected so much. How was I to define these concepts of love and comfort outside of what I witnessed?

Dr. Steve McKinion, professor of Theology and Patristics at Southeastern Baptist Theological Seminary, says the following regarding two people joined together in marriage:

The funny thing about marriage is that you cannot go anywhere when you mess up. And the only way to stick around is to forgive. This isn't like working a job. You can't leave. Marriage is all about forgiving and being forgiven. Marriage is such a laboratory for the gospel because sin and forgiveness happen constantly. This is such a picture of the truth of Christ for children.21

Marriage helps children.

It helps children understand and process. It helps us to see Scripture lived out and embodied. Throughout the Scriptures, it does not tell us how to have a happy home. When we read the text as it should be read, we understand that Scripture is about God reconciling the world to Himself through His Righteous Son, Christ. It is the act of believing this that makes a happy home. This is what sustains our families when everything goes downhill. Believing and resting in the gospel, the truth of Christ according to the Scriptures, fixes our families' unrighteousness and unfaithfulness.

More importantly, this is what sustains children when we desperately want answers and when we battle with the broken state of our families.

A counselor will not do this.

A conference will not do this.

A self-help program will not do this.

A book will not do this.

We must understand that a book is not the answer to our pain. It is not someone's advice that has saving power. A book will not bring true, lasting hope. But the good news is that we know Who can. We must come to the true realization that our situations are not hopeless, that the tomb is empty and God's plan to rescue and redeem His creation is underway - and has been throughout the existence of time.

But if you are a Christian, whether you are a 30-year veteran or a first-year rookie in the minors, this can still be hard to grasp at times. It's hard at night when you are falling asleep in your own tears and all you want is a hug. You're yearning for dad or mom to walk in and rub your back, to let you know everything is going to be alright. But they're not there. It's hard because you want to feel something. You want a person. You want someone tangible, someone you can touch, someone who audibly speaks to you. You want someone who hugs, someone who kisses, someone who sings you to sleep, and someone who dries your tears.

You want someone there.

Someone present.

Trust that the Spirit of God is present. He alone is the Great Comforter. He alone grants true peace and calm from life's raging, confusing, relentless storms. Trust that you have not been left. Believe that you have not been abandoned. In all of this, believe that there is more great news. We know that one day Christ will come again and make all things new. We know He will come and wipe away every tear.

Believe and trust in the glorious fact that God and God alone restores and rebuilds emotional and physical ruins. Only God can raise dead and decaying hearts and lives to life.

True Life.

He does.

And He will.

TRUST

I remember getting to my breaking point. The weight of my past was too heavy to carry anymore. I had been to counselor after counselor and I was tired. I was exhausted from carrying around this emotional boulder. I didn't want to let it go. I thought if I did I'd forget about him or that it'd look like I didn't care about him or still love him. I didn't want any of that.

But I was weak.

And I remember being on my knees early one morning, tears on my face and on the carpet, softly praying these words:

Okay Lord. I open up my hands and give this to You. I do not know Your ways for they are beyond me. I do not know Your thoughts for they are above mine. I trust You with my life and know Your Word says Your desire is to prosper me, to give me hope and a future. So Lord, I step out in faith not only to believe in You, but to believe You.

That was the hardest thing for me to do. It almost felt impossible to let go of my curiosity that wanted to know if things could have ended up differently for my family. But I wanted to believe God's restoration of my heart was possible.

Through it all, I realized how much bondage I was in. I was a slave. I was a slave to the memory of him and the memories of what went wrong when I was little and the memories of how I was treated.

More than that, I was a slave to the lack of memories.

I was chained to longings of wanting him there and wishing he had been different and aching for a normal childhood timeline. I didn't understand that this was going on in my heart. I was unaware of the grip all of this had on my emotions and thoughts.

But all of that was before lunch at Hardee's.

Sitting in our red and white booth, Matt looked at me before taking a bite of his Frisco Burger and asked me how I was doing. He wanted to know how I was processing everything connected to dad and the phone call and us not speaking. I told him I was fine and that things were as good as they could be for the time. I told him I was struggling with some things and that, for me, these struggles were things that I blamed on my dad's actions.

I truly thought that if it weren't for his departure and poor decisions these issues would be non-existent for me. As Matt listened, he sat back, deep in thought. He leaned forward, up against our table with his arms crossed, and said:

You know, your dad is only responsible for one thing: leaving your family.

Do you realize it is your responsibility for how you deal with that?

All my life I wanted to blame my dad for my inadequacies, my insecurities, my shame, my fear, my anger, my life. But it was in a Hardee's when the Lord knocked me out of that world and into reality. He broke me down.

I realized it was on me.

I realized my outlook on things was my fault and mine alone. It was sin in me to shift the blame from where it belonged. It was a complete re-evaluation. From there the Lord showed me that I must reframe the lies I once held as truth. It was a complete emotional and mental makeover.

If you are anything like me, you've held onto anger toward your parent that left and bitterness about your childhood for so long. You've held onto the search for answers surrounding the demise of your family. You've held onto these things for almost your entire life. And it's exhausting. But releasing isn't always easy. Letting go is hard. Letting go is work.

Letting go is trust.

Paul writes in the book of Romans that Abraham, one of the great patriarchs of the Old Testament, never doubted God.22 Paul says that Abraham was fully convinced that God was able to do exactly what He promised He would do. What was that exactly? That God would give Abraham and his wife a child. He knew God would come through. Despite Abraham's age and despite the bareness of Sarah's womb, it didn't matter. Their physical conditions and their circumstances didn't matter.

Abraham trusted. Abraham was confident.

Abraham believed God would come through on His promise that he and Sarah would bear a son.

These are strong statements concerning Abraham. The challenge is to ask if we are fully convinced in God's ability to do what He has promised us. Or, is our lack of trust making us waver? More importantly, is our lack of trust in Him causing us to believe things about Him that simply are not true, things that are contradictory to the message we have in the Scriptures?

Do we stand firm on the truth that God's ability to heal and restore is infinitely greater than our ability or our parents' ability to tear down and destroy?

The great news for us as children of God is that the Bible confirms for us that the One abiding in us is so much greater than the forces at work in the world and the forces at work in our families. We must believe that at every moment our Heavenly Father is up to something good for us, His children. I understand that it's far from easy. I understand at times you don't want to surrender. I understand that you want to know what happened. I understand you want to know why it had to be your family and not your neighbor's family.

I understand.

I understand because letting go of these things was the hardest thing I have ever done.

Through pain and tears and times of great suffering, I was forced to learn and claim that Christ is infinitely more concerned with the condition and health of my soul than He is with my physical discomfort. The truth is, many times He brings about physical discomfort and pain for His greater purpose to bring spiritual healing and spiritual formation. Christ is in the business of getting His children to understand that He is enough and that His very presence brings restoration and fulfillment to our greatest problems.

My journey and desperate search for answers, fueled by lifelong questions and doubts, always left me where I didn't want to be. It always left me empty handed. It was for my good and my joy that I traded in my journey for answers about my family's past for a journey that led to The Answer. And that's right where I need to be; on a road that leads to The Hope, not on a road that leads to a hope. It is this Hope, this Answer, that will endure till the end when everything else crumbles.

Despite what we see and experience, we desperately want our Heavenly Father to be different from the negative circumstances, ridden with sin that we find ourselves in and surrounded by. We deeply desire Him to be different from what we experience from sinful human beings, including ourselves. While it's hard for us to trust others, we want to trust Him. While it's hard for us to love others, we so much want to love Him. We want to believe that the sinful man or woman we are doesn't matter to Him. We want to believe that what we've done doesn't matter to Him and what matters is what He has done by putting sin to death and death to defeat. We want to believe that He, above all things and all people, is different from what we know.

We need hope in Someone greater than those who walk alongside us in this life. Nothing we can conceive matters because our conceptions are ruined by deception of our humanity; the deception we know that is caused by the infection of sin. We are constantly deceived to believe that He is, in fact, like all other things in this world that fail us. We are fooled to believe He is someone who will lure us into a scheme, only to take what He needs and leave. We fall prey to the lie that He is someone who says one thing only to do another; someone who says He will stick around but leaves the next morning before we wake up.

Friend, never believe that God is unable to take our negative misconceptions of Him and infuse us with clarity from His Spirit that dispels those lies. We must not let human ailments be ascribed to One who is far beyond us. Neither our faults nor those of our parents will ever transfer over to Him.

Never.

He is the only Father incapable of leaving.

Even when life feels dark and you can't see. Even when you're tossed around, beaten and battered from the jolts of situations and circumstances. Even when life feels too much like a frightening roller coaster going 200 miles per hour, flipping you upside down and inside out.

Because sometimes life feels like those roller coasters we talked about earlier.

Life rises and it falls. It has

Ups.

Downs.

Turns.

Jolts.

Twists.

Loops.

And there may be some aspects of life that have the same concepts of a roller coaster, but in reality, life is quite different from everyone's theme park favorite.

Life is vastly different because we can't stand on the ground and look up and know the twists and turns and upside-down loops that are going to come in our lives tomorrow or the next day. If we could, we'd avoid them every chance we could. We'd avoid our parents leaving us. We'd avoid getting cancer. We'd avoid having to watch struggle and hardship. But we don't know every bend and curve in the track. We don't know where our lives are going to go or when they'll slow down or when they'll pick up speed or when they'll rise or when they'll fall. Unlike a roller coaster, we have no idea what to expect on a minute by minute, second by second basis.

This is hard for us.

This is not fun for us.

Especially when the ride hurts.

Because what makes a roller coaster exhilarating, its twists, loops, speed, turns, climbs, and steep descents, are the very things that make life so tough and unpleasant at times. The aspects that make a roller coaster fun do the very opposite to our journeys in life.

When life takes unexpected drops and turns it pains us. It's not exciting. It's uncomfortable. We wish we could get off and we want the ride to end. We want to open our eyes and for it all to be over.

We feel sick.

But what happens when we get to these twists and turns? What happens next? How do we keep going?

The question for all of us comes down to an issue of safety and security. It comes down to that very uncomfortable bar that presses on our chest too tightly and the seatbelt that cuts across our lap. It comes down to our protection. What's holding us in? What's keeping us safely positioned in our seat when the car goes upside down and barrel rolls?

For us, this is where the truth of Scripture is so important.

We must be self-reflecting and ask ourselves what is securing us. If it's our own vices then at the first drop of the coaster, we're gone. We're falling out. If it's finding answers to why our parents got a divorce and why one of them isn't around anymore, if that's what is keeping us in and keeping us going, we will never last.

We won't survive.

But if we are strapped in and secured by the truth of His Word and His promises, that He will never leave us, that He loves us, that He wants our good, that He is trustworthy, that He is just, that He is in control, then things are going to be far better for us. When we don't want to secure ourselves with Scripture and what God says, it's because we think God is doing what that ruler is doing. We think He is keeping us from something for no good reason. We think He is strict and just out to get us. We think He just doesn't want us to have fun or doesn't want us to do anything exciting. We think he is against us.

This couldn't be further from the truth.

We need to be secure in the grand reality that God has not given up on the world and that includes us and our families. We need to trust that He knows everything about the roller coaster He's built. He knows every bolt, screw, beam, wheel, twist, turn, loop, speed, rise, and fall.

And He knows us.

Let the truth of the Scripture cover us with peace to know that, if we believe and trust that Jesus is who He says He is and that He did what He said He would do, there's no way we're falling out of the car. We're strapped in. We're secure. We're safe.

Yes, the ride will get bumpy.

It will get rough.

It will get winding.

It will get turned upside down.

It will get twisted.

But through it all don't despair. He's got you. He built the entire thing.

It is this saving and joyous truth that my mom wanted us to rest in and find assurance and security in above anything and everything else. She wanted us aware of who God is and how trustworthy He is. She wanted us strapped in and kept tight.

After my dad packed up and left, she wasted no time stepping in and dedicating all she had to our family. She knew it would be hard. She knew it was going to be exhausting. She knew the journey would be long. But she did everything she could to make sure we knew she loved us more than her life.

There was never a wasted opportunity to hug us,

to be available to us,

to tell us how much she cared for us,

to tell us how much she loved us,

to make sure we knew that she was for us.

My mom wanted us to know, trust, and believe that she was fighting for us and for what was left of our family. She was on her face daily before our Sovereign Father, our Holy King, our Righteous Protector, exchanging her energy for His breath and His life. She knew she didn't have what it would take for the days and years ahead but she did know that her Savior and Lord was

a Rescuer,

a Helper,

a Provider,

a Healer,

and a Father.

These were things that on her own she could not give. She knew more than anyone in our family that a returning father or husband would not make things better. She knew it was the saving grace and mercy of the Almighty that would bring peace, comfort, and wholeness.

The arms of the True Father were what she knew her broken and hurting sons and daughter needed. I am beyond grateful for the faithful life my mother lives. Without question, as I have mentioned already, she is the most incredible human being I have ever known. I will always be thankful for how she consistently, without fail, laid the lives of my brother, sister, and me before the Father's throne daily and continues to do so to this day.

The fact is, what if you never discover a single answer behind your parents' divorce? Will you trust that His ways are beyond you? If we hope to have joy in this life we must release those questions to the Lord's hand. We must be okay with never being able to solve our families' mysteries. In the end, what do we believe we gain? We may answer with words such as "comfort" or "rest," but it is only union with the Resurrected Jesus that brings those things. When we require an answer from the Lord, it merely shows our lack of trust in Him to do what He promised and a lack of belief that He is who He has revealed Himself to be.

Because He is a restorer.

He is a comforter.

And He is a healer.

He has brought seasons of healing over time to my aged wounds. He has been faithful to rebuild and restore my heart with Himself and nothing else. It was in 2012 that He took me down a road to healing that I didn't know if I was ready for. I was scared and afraid about what would happen. And through it all, it revealed stale feelings of bitterness and hurt tucked so deeply down in my soul I didn't even know they were there.

HEART SURGERY

There I sat in Dave's office.

Dave wanted to ask me some questions about my family and wanted me to share with him how I processed everything that happened over the years in regards to my father. He wanted to know how I thought I was dealing with it at the time. Dave didn't know much, but he wanted to know more. He wanted to make sure I was okay. He wanted to make sure my heart was healthy.

I began to share openly and honestly with him, explaining what had transpired over the years. It was hard revisiting those ruins. I still didn't like the fact that my dad made me hurt. Dave and I continued to process these things together. He was committed to exploring the depths of these aches with me, longing for Jesus to mend these wounds and fill my broken heart with Himself. We prayed that God give me a new heart for my dad. We prayed earnestly for a heart ravaged by the corrosion of anger and bitterness to be washed clean, restored, renewed, and cleansed by the forgiving love of Christ.

It wasn't easy.

We spent months dialoguing together and walking through old storerooms of memories. I prayed expectantly for the Lord to renew my heart and my affections for my dad. I prayed expectantly for Him to heal old wounds and fill old cracks in my heart with His endless rushing rivers of grace and mercy and forgiveness.

On my face I prayed for a new spirit. I knew that He alone was able to give me strength and do graciously beyond all that I asked and could ever imagine in regards to my relationship and personal demons with my dad. I prayed the Lord would perform extensive open-heart surgery on me. I desperately wanted and needed Him to stitch up every valve that leaked hatred or disgust for my dad into my mind, soul, and heart. I simply asked, on my knees, for the Lord to give me a heart and eyes that looked on my father with the same affection and extravagant love that Christ does. I wanted my heart for my dad to be like His heart for my dad.

I wanted a gracious heart.

A forgiving heart.

A merciful heart.

A loving heart.

I needed this kind of heart and I knew that it was only by the grace and power of the Spirit that it would happen.

I knew God was able, and I knew I wasn't.

I needed the Lord to do in my heart what I knew was impossible for me to do on my own power: to truly forgive my dad. I knew forgiving him would free me from years of bondage. I knew forgiving him was the Lord's will for my life. I knew forgiving him was the Lord's mandate from His Word. I knew forgiving him was acting in obedience toward my Heavenly Father. I knew forgiving him was action flowing from the belief and understanding that my own sin was just as vile in the sight of a Holy God as my dad's. In fact, I understood the wretchedness of my actions towards God was infinitely greater than the wretchedness of my dad's toward me. I understood that without Christ, I was an enemy of God and a rebel towards Him.

I began to understand that I didn't have any justice to seek, that true justice was God's. I understood that my primary concern is that I am a sinner in need of constant grace and mercy. I understood that the only thing lovely about me in God's eyes is the radiance and splendor of His Son. Christ, and Christ alone, is my hope of righteousness and glory. I needed to believe and hold fast to the truth that the saving work of Christ's life, death, and resurrection was not needed to atone for just the wrong others committed against me. Rather, it was also needed to atone for the wrong I committed against a Holy and Righteous God.

Reconciliation with my dad ceased to be my primary concern because I longed for his reconciliation with the Father so much more.

Our relationship is temporary. It is finite. It is passing. His relationship with the One True God, made possible only by the saving work of Christ, is eternal. Without the understanding and acceptance of Christ's work on the cross, my dad's relationship with the Lord is far more bruised, broken, and fractured than his and mine will ever be. More importantly, the consequences of a broken relationship with his Heavenly Father are infinitely more severe. I have spent countless mornings on my face crying tears of burning desire, asking the Lord to save my father's soul. I tell the Lord constantly that I don't care if my relationship with my dad is ever mended, but ask that He would graciously, in His infinite mercy and power, draw my dad's heart to Himself.

Being separated from my dad while I walk this earth is nothing compared to my dad being eternally separated from an Almighty God, the Sole Creator and Sustainer of all things.

Walking under the weight of this truth changed my life. The Lord released me from over a decade of emotional bondage and baggage by showing me more of Himself. Jesus rebuilt and restored this part of my heart and has been abundantly gracious. I am overwhelmed with gratitude by the grace He continues to give. It never fails to be more than enough.

He never fails to be more than enough.

Every day He continues to bring healing. There are days that are harder than others, but I understand this to be a lifelong marathon with extensive rehabilitation, not a three-month sprint capped off with a Buzz Lightyear Band-Aid. I understand on certain days there will be more walking than running. There will even be days of tear-drenched crawling. It will be difficult to take in if he is not among family and close friends in the hospital waiting room, anxiously ready to hear my newborn's cries. What I fear most is gaining word of his death through handed down information. I fear never again getting to exchange words with him. I would love to simply hear his voice again.

As Dave and I reflected on my dad's silent absence throughout the years, we also reflected on mine.

He asked me to prayerfully consider what it would look like to be the first to make a move. He wanted me to think about what it would look like for me to step forward in an attempt to open communication again with my dad. After all we saw the Lord do in my heart, Dave asked me to pray towards seeking reconciliation with my dad after all these years. Now that this was something I held with an open hand as opposed to clutching it tightly in bitterness, we proceeded to prayerfully take steps in this direction.

It wasn't long before I knew deep down in the marrow of my bones that this was the appropriate action to take. I realized those past eight years for me were stained with pride. I had refused to be the one to contact him. Why should it be me? I wasn't the one who left. I wasn't the one who was angry.

But I was.

My refusal to contact my dad over the years was far from anything resembling Christ's lengthy and deliberate pursuit of my own soul. Christ pursued me in the thickness of my rebellion when I wanted nothing to do with His love. I realized that I must pursue my dad in this very same way and with the same intentionality. I realized that forgiveness must look past wrong done and present faults. After all, that is how God came to us and this is how He relates to us still.

Only by the working of His grace in my life was I able to move forward with a healed heart. In February of 2012, I secured my dad's mailing address and sent him the following words:

Dad,

There may be some form of words that I could come up with to begin this letter but I don't think I would ever find them. To be honest, I don't know how to start a letter to someone that I have failed to speak to for so long. Someone better with words could maybe come up with something. And out of all the things to say I don't know if any is more important than this simple truth: I miss you. And I'm sorry that it has been this long since we last spoke. I simply cannot believe it's 2012 and it was in 2004 that we last exchanged words. I feel terrible. I am sorry if I ever made you believe that I did not want to talk to you or see you. There has never been a day pass that I did not wonder what you were doing or where you were.

I don't know what has kept me from writing you all these years. Maybe fear. Maybe pride. Maybe uncertainty. I don't know. But one thing I do know is that I am deeply sorry for standing back in the shadows and not stepping out and writing you or calling. I guess what I feared the most is what on earth I would say. There were so many things that I could say but didn't know which things to choose. I would have wanted to tell you about college, graduating from college, almost getting engaged, releasing a CD, starting grad school. There were so many things I wanted you to know but didn't know how to tell you.

I wanted to know what you were doing. How work was going, where you were living, how was Hershey, and so many other things.

With all of this, I just wanted you to know that I miss you. I want you to know that I love you and would love to know how you are doing. Again, I am so sorry that I have waited this long to make an effort to get in touch with you. Please forgive me.

I love you more than you know and I hope more than anything to hear from you soon. But if not, that's okay too. I just wanted you to know that I have been thinking about you and missing you for so long.

Love you Dad.

I wish I could tell you that I heard back from him within that week but I didn't. Even more I wish I could say I heard back from him period. But I haven't.

And that's okay.

I'm okay.

Christ is still sovereign and He is still good.

Writing those words is one thing but believing them is something different entirely. It is the goodness and mercy of God that allows me to release this situation and place it in His hands and at His feet.

God's grace and mercy are so freeing for our souls. They allow us to breathe underneath the wreckage of the sin in our lives and the sin entangling this world. It is God's mercy that gave me new eyes to see the darkness of my own heart and its effect on how I viewed the brokenness of my family. It is God's goodness that gave me new eyes to see my dad. It is God's grace that gave me a new heart that brewed new affections for my father.

This new heart and these new affections radically changed the way I understood the reality of my home as a child and my desire to tell my story. I no longer wanted to use these words to hurt, but rather to heal.

Because Jesus desires restoration for all His children.

And wherever you are right now, maybe on your lunch break in your car or quietly in the back corner of the library while you're studying or maybe on the way to the grocery store or J. Crew or Urban Outfitters - trust that. Trust that he desires to restore and renew.

Because whatever the case may be and whatever your story is, these pages have been my story and the reality is that it's not just my story.

My story is the story of many.

And that story is one from inside the dark corners of a soul that many keep secret

LEFT

and silent.

That story is one from a kid who didn't want it.

A story he didn't write.

A story she didn't choose.

A story that is affecting an entire generation.

The story of a generation left on the front porch.

Because the reason I began writing this years ago and the reason I wanted to share my story was because my life hurt. It wasn't fun and I knew others felt the same way about their own. It's because for so long I understood abandonment. I knew in my bones what it felt like. I knew deep down in my soul what it was and how hard it punched.

Being left and being traded and being substituted made sense to me. In fact, it made too much sense to me.

I understood that people leave.

Father.

Mother.

Husband.

Wife.

Abandonment happens every day in every way. There is no question about this. Not one. No one disagrees and no one contests. The question we must wrestle with is, what do we do after abandonment strikes? Many give up. We become empty. We lose hope. We become angry. There's not even hope of having any sign of hope to come. There is no doubt this is how we feel. Our lives, our stories, and our abandonment are real. It is ever-present. It looms over us and it quickly becomes our world. Not because we desire it and not because we want to carry it around in our pockets or around our necks.

Not at all.

It's because of the simple fact that our trust has been shattered. Our security has been broken. Our lives have been turned in every direction and we have not a clue how to get them back to the way they were. The question has been posed, who can we run to? Who is it that we can trust? Who will be our advocate? Who is it that will put our shattered pieces back together? Who can we rest in to know they will not open the door and leave us in the middle of the night? Again, who will fight for us?

There is great news for us as children of the Perfect Father. Because of Jesus, there is no more longing and no more uncertainty. If the Blood of the Lamb has washed us, our wounds have been healed solely because of the wounds He was given. Our hurts have been covered. Our worth has been secured. Our lives have been rescued. Our souls have been purchased. We have been fought for and we have been won!

This Great News, this Answer, this Redeemer, this Seed, this Hope, has a name.

His name is Jesus.

He is the Christ.

He is the fulfillment of the Old Testament promises.

Through it all, the true aftermath of our situations is so incredibly sweet and savoring because when we hit the bottom of our pit, our only hope is to look up. When we do just that, we see the ever-so-satisfying and perfected love of our Pursuer.

He is our Savior.

He is our Rescuer.

He is the Lover of our souls.

It is He who came to rescue us and never leave us.

He came to save, not to condemn.

He is the only Answer and Hope for our brokenness and our emptiness.

He fills and He refills and He fulfills.

He alone.

Jesus.

L|E

EPILOGUE
MEMORY

Memories.

They can be good.

And they can be bad.

They can hurt.

And they can make you laugh.

There is a lot that we want to remember in our lives and a lot that we wish we could forget. There are many stories out there in this world. Many similar to the one I have used these pages to tell. That's because we all have memories that are like this. We all have stories like this.

We all have stories that aren't fun.

Stories that are filled with pain.

Stories that are filled with depression.

Stories that are filled with anger.

Stories that are filled with bitterness.

Stories that are filled with uncertainty.

Stories that are filled with insecurity.

Stories that are filled with loneliness.

And we all have ways of remembering different parts and different chapters of these stories. We might use bookshelves. We might use polar bears. Or we might keep a book on our coffee table. We make these little monuments to remember and rewind.

To keep certain memories alive.

To keep certain people around.

Throughout the Scriptures we see so many accounts of God's people building altars and giving them names describing what the Lord had done at that point in time and at that place. These were reminders for them for not only what God had done but Who He was and is.

There have been seasons of my life, some long and some short, where I cared more about reminders and signs of my dad's existence than I did about the existence and presence of Jesus. I cared more about erecting monuments and altars that showed me who my dad was and that he did exist and that he was real and that he was around for a while. But how that failed me. How that did not do for my heart what I believed it would.

It took me to places that were empty.

Instead of spending our lives and our hearts' energy constructing altars and monuments for things that will continue to leave us empty, may we be so led to build towering representations and reminders of God's presence throughout our lives and His constant faithfulness and goodness. We need Him more than anything. We need to fill ourselves up with memories, thoughts, and reminders of His greatness, goodness, and faithfulness. We need to be reminded of these things more than we need to be reminded of anything else. Let us look and recall the things He has done and the grace and mercy He has showered upon us.

The good news is that He will always come through.

He never changes.

He will never fail.

That's joyful news for the brokenhearted.

And that's all of us.

L|TY

Much Love to Those Who Were A Part of This

MOM for being the absolute greatest.

STU for being the best big brother during high and low times.

GRACIE for always being there to laugh with and cry with.

AUNT B for everything.

RUSTY for caring and loving our crazy family so sacrificially.

ATWOODS for your green couch and sailboat sheets.

STEVE TURNER for your years of investment and godly leadership.

DAVID HORNER for your pastoral care and wealth of encouragement.

TREVIN WAX for believing in this project.

BRANDON SMITH for making the last push for this manuscript.

AUNT SHARON for your guidance and so many loving phone calls.

WHITNEY, JUDY, & CINDY for your hours of edits.

TIM for being a rock to lean on in the gym, doctor's office, and at work.

CITY CHURCH for being a family that believes Jesus changes it all.

RAINER PUBLISHING for getting this into people's hands

KATHERINE for your forgiveness, your love, your care, and your sacrifice.

●●●●　　●

●●●●　●

ABOUT THE AUTHOR

Jonathan Edwards (M.Div, Th.M) has served churches in various roles for the past 10 years, from music and creative arts/graphic design to serving and equipping college students. He is currently the Director of Curriculum for Docent Research Group, where he also serves as a lead writer. He and his wife, Katherine, live in the Raleigh/Durham area of North Carolina, where he is pursuing his Ph.D at Southeastern Baptist Theological Seminary. Read more of his writing at NotThePuritan.com.

L|E

···· ·

ENDNOTES

1   Genesis 2:18-23

2   Genesis 3:-13

3   Genesis 3:15

4   Revelation 21:3-5

5   *Father Fiction* by Donald Miller released in 2010, published by Howard Books. This was a re-release of Miller's 2006 *To Own A Dragon*.

6   Nehemiah 1:1-3

7   Excerpt taken from Charles Swindoll's *Come Before Winter and Share My Hope* on p. 231. Published in 1994 by Zondervan.

8   Proverbs 20:7

9   Deuteronomy 6:4-9

10 Deuteronomy 6:20-24

11 Psalm 78:2-8

12 David Kinnaman's *You Lost Me: Why Young Christians Are Leaving Church... And Rethinking Faith* was published by Baker Books in 2011.

13 C.S. Lewis, "First and Second Things," in *God in the Dock: Essays on Theology and Ethics*. Published by Eerdmans in 1994.

14 Quote taken from Haim G. Ginott's *Teacher and Child: A Book for Parents and Teachers*, published by Scribner Paper Fiction in 1993.

15 Quote take from Chap Clark's *Hurt*, released in 2004 under Baker Academic.

16 Quote taken from John Eldredge's *Wild At Heart*. Published in 2001 Thomas Nelson.

17 Luke 15

18 Quote taken from Chap Clark's *Hurt*, released in 2004 under Baker Academic.

19 A.W. Tozer's *Knowledge of the Holy* was published in 1961 under Harper-Collins.

20 This excerpt from Paul Tripp is taken from his weekly email send-out, Wednesday's Word. This particular section was sent on July 25, 2012. For more information on Paul Tripp's ministry, visit www.PaulTripp.com

21 Dr. Steve McKinion explained this during class on August 29, 2012. This particular lecture was during Theology III at Southeastern Baptist Theological Seminary.

22 Romans 4

Made in the USA
Lexington, KY
18 January 2019